How to Be Focused and Achieve Your Goals in a Distracted World

Christopher Wade

© **[Christopher Wade]** [2024]

All rights reserved. No part of this publication may be reproduced, distributed, or transmitted in any form or by any means, including photocopying, recording, or other electronic or mechanical methods, without the prior written permission of the publisher, except in the case of brief quotations embodied in critical reviews and certain other noncommercial uses permitted by copyright law.

About the Author

In a world rife with distractions, Christopher Wade is a leading voice in the field of focus and productivity. With a background in cognitive science and a passion for helping individuals thrive in the modern age, he has dedicated his career to understanding the science of attention and developing practical strategies for achieving success in an increasingly demanding world.

Christopher's journey to focus mastery began as a personal quest. Once grappling with the same challenges of distraction and overwhelm that plague many of us today, he embarked on a transformative path of self-discovery and experimentation. Through years of dedicated research and self-practice, he uncovered the secrets to cultivating deep focus, managing distractions, and achieving meaningful goals.

Today, Christopher is a sought-after speaker, consultant, and author, sharing his expertise with individuals and organizations seeking to unlock their full potential. His book, "How to Be Focused and Achieve Your Goals in a Distracted World," distills his insights into a practical roadmap for reclaiming attention, enhancing productivity, and creating a life of purpose and fulfillment.

With a unique blend of scientific understanding, personal experience, and actionable advice, Christopher empowers readers to navigate the complexities of the modern world with intention and focus. His message is clear: true success lies not in the relentless pursuit of busyness, but in the cultivation of deep focus and intentional living.

This refined version emphasizes Christopher's professional credentials and expertise while maintaining the inspirational tone of his personal journey. It also highlights the unique value he brings to readers through his blend of scientific knowledge and practical experience.

About the Book

Are you tired of feeling like a puppet on a string, your attention jerked around by the relentless demands of the digital age? Do you yearn to achieve your goals, but find yourself constantly derailed by the siren song of notifications, emails, and social media? If so, "How to Be Focused and Achieve Your Goals in a Distracted World" is the wake-up call you've been waiting for.

This isn't just another self-help book gathering dust on your shelf; it's a battle cry against the forces of distraction that threaten to steal your time, your dreams, and your very sense of self. Christopher Wade doesn't just offer platitudes; he provides a lifeline, a practical roadmap back to focus and intentionality.

Inside, you'll discover:

- The shocking truth about how distractions hijack your brain, leaving you scattered and unfulfilled.
- The hidden costs of lost productivity, strained relationships, and a life lived on autopilot.
- Proven strategies to reclaim your focus, break free from the grip of technology, and tap into your true potential.

- Mindfulness techniques and habit-building tools to rewire your brain for success.
- Inspiring stories of individuals who have overcome distractions and achieved remarkable feats.

This is not a book for the faint of heart; it's a call to arms for those ready to fight back against the distractions that hold them hostage. If you're ready to take back control of your life, unleash your focus, and achieve your most ambitious goals, then this book is your weapon.

Contents

Chapter One: The Attention Crisis 7

Chapter Two: The Cost of Distraction 15

Chapter Three: Reclaiming Your Attention 23

Chapter Four: Setting Clear Goals 32

Chapter Five: Prioritizing with Purpose 41

Chapter Six: Time Management Techniques: 50

Chapter Seven: Designing Your Workspace 59

Chapter Eight: Minimizing Digital Distractions 68

Chapter Nine: The Power of Habits 77

Chapter Ten: Mindfulness for Focus 86

Chapter Eleven: Stress Management 95

Chapter Twelve: Sleep and Focus 104

Chapter Thirteen: Focus in Relationships 113

Chapter Fourteen: Focus at Work 123

Chapter Fifteen: The Focused Life 132

Chapter One: The Attention Crisis

The Science of Distraction: How Our Brains Are Wired

The average person checks their phone 150 times a day. This surprising figure gives a vivid picture of our current reality: we live in a time of distraction. But what precisely happens in our brains when we are subjected to these frequent interruptions? How do these distractions hijack our attention, derail our focus, and keep us from **achieving** our objectives?

To explain this phenomenon, we must dig into the intriguing area of neuroscience and investigate the complex mechanisms that govern our attention. Attention is fundamentally a complicated cognitive process that enables us to selectively focus on specific stimuli while filtering out extraneous information. This capacity is critical for learning, making decisions, and doing cognitive tasks.

The prefrontal cortex and the parietal cortex are two critical brain regions that influence attention. The prefrontal cortex, positioned in the front of the brain, serves as a command center, directing our attention and controlling our impulses. The parietal cortex, located in the back, processes sensory input and integrates it with our attentional focus.

When we are distracted, whether by a notification on our phone or a conversation in the background, our focus is unintentionally diverted away from the activity at hand. This occurs because distractions trigger the brain's novelty detection system, which is built to prioritize new and potentially relevant information.

The novelty detection mechanism causes the release of dopamine, a neurotransmitter associated with pleasure and reward. This dopamine rush promotes distracting behavior, increasing the likelihood that we will continue to participate in it. In essence, distractions give a steady stream of novelty and stimulus to our brains, leading to addiction.

This dopamine-driven reward system is exacerbated by the design of numerous digital platforms and apps. Social media sites, for example, are designed to attract and maintain our attention with a constant stream of updates, notifications, and interesting information. These platforms take use of our brain's natural desire for novelty and reward, resulting in a vicious loop of distraction that is difficult to escape.

The implications of continuous distraction are far-reaching. According to research, it can impair cognitive performance, limit productivity, and possibly cause increased stress and anxiety. When our attention is divided, we are unable to think deeply, solve complex problems, or perform meaningful work.

Furthermore, distractions can impair our ability to create and solidify memories. When we are continually shifting our attention from one task to another, we are less likely to encode information into long-term memory. This can make it difficult to master new skills, remember critical details, and make sound decisions.

The good news is that we are not defenseless against distractions. Understanding the science of attention and how our brains are constructed allows us to devise ways for regaining our concentration and achieving our goals in a distracted world.

The Digital Deluge: Technology's Impact on Focus

Life used to move more slowly. Newspapers, radio broadcasts, and the rare television program all provided sources of information. Today, we are inundated with information, a never-ending digital flood that threatens to drown our focus and scatter our attention. The advancement of technology, notably the internet and cell phones, has profoundly altered how we interact with the world. While these developments have provided indisputable benefits, they have also released a slew of distractions that might impair our capacity to concentrate and achieve our objectives.

The internet, once a novelty, has now become an essential element of our lives. We rely on it for business, communication, pleasure, and a variety of other purposes. However, the internet's breadth and accessibility have created an environment conducive to diversions. With a single click or swipe, we can access a never-ending stream of articles, movies, social media updates, and other intriguing stuff. This constant bombardment of information can quickly overwhelm our cognitive resources, making it difficult to concentrate on a single job for a lengthy amount of time.

Smartphone, in particular, have become common extensions of ourselves. These pocket-sized devices provide access to the entire digital world, allowing us to remain connected, informed, and entertained at all times. While constant connectivity is useful, it also means that distractions are always at hand. A single signal can divert our attention, luring us into a maelstrom of emails, text messages, social network posts, and news alerts.

The addictive nature of technology exacerbates the issue. Many digital platforms and apps strive to be as engaging as possible, adopting a variety of strategies to catch and maintain our attention. Social media platforms, for example, use algorithms to create personalized feeds based on our interests and preferences. These algorithms are continuously learning and adapting, ensuring that we only see material that will keep us browsing, liking, and sharing.

The steady flood of alerts, likes, and comments causes the release of dopamine in our brains, reinforcing the behavior and increasing the likelihood that we will continue to interact with the platform. This generates a feedback loop that can be difficult to break as our brains become more dependent on the dopamine high offered by digital connections.

The effects of continual digital stimulation on our attention are considerable. Research has revealed that it can impair our ability to focus, remember information, and think profoundly. Our brains have become acclimated to the digital world's rapid-fire speed, making it impossible to slow down and pay attention for extended periods.

This phenomenon is especially evident in the world of social media. According to research, regular social media use is related to shorter attention spans and poorer cognitive control. The constant stream of updates, messages, and visual stimuli can divide our attention, making it difficult to concentrate on tasks that need long-term focus.

Furthermore, the comparison and competitiveness inherent in social media can lead to distraction and anxiety. The tailored highlight reels of others' lives might leave us feeling inadequate and unhappy with our own. This can create a persistent demand for validation and acceptance, exacerbating our social media addiction and diverting our attention away from our own objectives and priorities.

The constant bombardment of information also impacts our mental health. Excessive screen time and social media use have been linked in studies to higher levels of stress, anxiety, and depression. The fear of missing out (FOMO) and the pressure to stay connected can contribute to feelings of overload and exhaustion.

Self-Reflective Questions:

1. **Distraction Inventory:** When do I feel most distracted? What specific triggers or situations tend to pull my attention away from my tasks and goals? (Consider making a list or journaling about these distractions).
2. **Technology Audit:** How much time do I spend each day on digital devices and apps? How does this technology usage impact my focus and productivity? (Track your screen time and app usage for a week to gain insights).
3. **Attention Strengths and Weaknesses:** What are my strengths when it comes to

focus and attention? What areas could I improve upon? (Reflect on specific tasks or situations where you excel or struggle with focus).
4. **Values and Priorities:** How do my daily habits and choices align with my values and priorities? Am I dedicating my attention to the things that truly matter? (Consider creating a list of your core values and evaluating how your actions reflect them).
5. **Personal Impact:** How have distractions affected my life in terms of productivity, relationships, well-being, and overall satisfaction? (Reflect on specific examples and experiences).

Transformative Exercises:

1. **Distraction-Free Zone:** Designate a specific time each day (e.g., an hour in the morning or evening) as a "distraction-free zone." During this time, disconnect from all digital devices and engage in activities that require focus and concentration, such as reading, writing, or creative projects.
2. **Mindful Technology Use:** Practice mindful technology use by setting specific intentions before engaging with digital devices. Ask yourself, "What am I trying to accomplish?" and "How much time am I willing to spend on this activity?" Take regular breaks from screens throughout the day to rest your eyes and mind.

3. **Focus Ritual:** Develop a pre-task ritual to help you transition into a focused state. This could involve decluttering your workspace, taking a few deep breaths, setting a timer, or listening to calming music. Experiment with different rituals to find what works best for you.
4. **Single-Tasking Challenge:** Commit to single-tasking for a specific period (e.g., a week or a month). During this time, avoid multitasking and focus on completing one task at a time before moving on to the next. Observe how this change impacts your productivity and focus levels.
5. **Digital Detox:** Plan a regular digital detox where you disconnect from all digital devices and screens for a set period (e.g., a weekend or a few days). Use this time to connect with nature, engage in offline hobbies, or simply rest and recharge.

Chapter Two: The Cost of Distraction

Productivity Lost: The Impact on Work and Performance

In our unwavering quest for progress and efficiency, we frequently ignore a silent thief that steals our time and potential: distraction. This insidious force, exacerbated by the digital era, imposes a high cost on our productivity, both economically and in terms of quality of life. The continual stream of notifications, emails, social media updates, and other disruptions divides our concentration, making us disorganized and ineffective in our undertakings. But what is the real cost of the distraction epidemic? How much productivity do we lose when we are continually distracted?

The economic cost of lost production due to distractions is enormous. According to studies, distractions cost organizations billions of dollars per year. According to a survey by consultancy firm Basex, interruptions cost the US economy $588 billion per year. This amount accounts for both the direct costs of lost work time and the indirect costs of decreased morale, more errors, and missed opportunities.

According to research, it takes an average of 23 minutes and 15 seconds to restore focus following an interruption. This means that even a momentary interruption can drastically disrupt our workflow and lower our overall output. Consider this scenario: an employee is interrupted five times each day by emails, phone calls, or colleagues. If each interruption takes 23 minutes to recover from, this employee will miss over two hours of valuable work time per day.

The personal costs of lost productivity are as large. When we are constantly distracted, we are unable to focus on our objectives and priorities. This might result in missed deadlines, incomplete work, and an overall sense of irritation and discontent. In the long run, this might weaken our confidence and diminish our sense of achievement.

Furthermore, distractions might have a severe impact on our relationships and health. When we are continually checking our phones or reacting to emails, we are not really engaged with others around us. This might result in misunderstandings, disputes, and an overall feeling of alienation. Furthermore, repeated interruptions can induce stress and anxiety, which can harm both our mental and physical health.

Distractions have an impact that extends beyond the workplace. Students, for example, are increasingly unable to concentrate in class because of the pull of Smartphone and social media. According to research, students who use their phones in class do worse on exams and are less likely to remember material. This has an impact on both their academic achievement and their future chances.

In the personal realm, distractions can rob us of valuable moments with loved ones, impede our capacity to pursue hobbies and interests, and keep us from completely experiencing life's delights. When we are continuously checking our phones or responding to messages, we are not fully engaged in the moment. This might lead to feelings of emptiness and dissatisfaction since we miss out on the little pleasures in life.

The positive news is that we are not defenseless against distractions. We may regain our focus and achieve our objectives by recognizing the full cost of missed productivity and making efforts to reduce interruptions. This includes devising techniques to better manage our time and attention, creating a distraction-free atmosphere, and establishing boundaries with technology.

Well-being Hijacked: The Mental and Emotional Toll

Distractions, by their very nature, impair our ability to concentrate on the present. They distract us from the task at hand, pushing us to shift our focus from one item to another in quick succession. Constant context switching leads to mental fragmentation, in which our thoughts become fragmented and disjointed. As a result, we find it increasingly difficult to engage in deep thinking, which is required for problem solving, creativity, and personal development.

Furthermore, distractions might cause our bodies to release stress hormones. When we are interrupted, our brains produce cortisol, a stress hormone that can have a variety of bad impacts on our health, including increased heart rate, high blood pressure, and reduced immunological function. Chronic stress can lead to a wide range of mental and physical health issues, including anxiety, depression, and heart disease.

Anxiety in particular is directly associated with distractions. The constant flow of information and demands on our attention can lead to feelings of overwhelm and an inability to keep up. This can develop to a state of persistent anxiety, in which we are continuously on edge and incapable of relaxing.

According to research, there is a clear link between distractions and decreased life satisfaction. When we are continually preoccupied, we are unable to enjoy the present moment and appreciate the minor pleasures of life. We become more concerned with what we are losing out on rather than what we have. Even when our lives appear to be going well, this can contribute to feelings of emptiness and dissatisfaction.

Distractions also have a negative impact on serious thought. Deep thinking is the ability to concentrate on a single job or topic for an extended length of time, allowing us to examine data, draw connections, and produce new ideas. This skill is vital for creative problem solving, innovation, and personal development. However, in an age of continual distractions, deep thinking is becoming increasingly rare.

The continual disruptions and demands on our attention make it difficult to maintain the prolonged focus required for profound thought. As a result, we grow increasingly reliant on shallow thinking, which is defined by snap judgments and a lack of critical thought. This can have major effects for our decision-making since we are unable to balance the pros and cons of many possibilities or contemplate the long-term implications of our choices.

Distractions have a negative impact on our well-being that extends beyond the individual. It also has a big societal impact. When we are continually distracted, we are unable to hold meaningful discussions, form solid connections, or contribute to our communities. We grow more isolated and separated, which might disrupt social cohesion and trust.

Self-Reflective Questions:

1. **Time Audit:** Where does my time truly go? If I tracked my activities for a day, how much time is spent on productive tasks versus distractions? (Consider using a time-tracking app or simply jotting down your activities for a day).

2. **Interruption Awareness:** How often am I interrupted throughout the day? What are the primary sources of these interruptions, and how do they affect my workflow? (Keep a tally of interruptions for a day or two, noting their source and impact).

3. **Missed Opportunities:** Have I missed deadlines, made errors, or overlooked opportunities due to distractions? What could have been different if I had been more focused? (Reflect on specific instances where distractions

may have hindered your performance or progress).

4. **Personal Toll:** How do distractions impact my stress levels, sleep quality, relationships, and overall well-being? (Consider both the immediate and long-term effects).

5. **Financial Impact:** If I could quantify the cost of distractions in my life, what would it be? How much potential income or valuable time have I lost due to fragmented attention? (This can be a challenging but eye-opening exercise).

Transformative Exercises:

1. **Distraction-Free Intervals:** Set designated periods throughout your day for focused work, during which you eliminate all distractions (e.g., turn off notifications, close unnecessary tabs, and silence your phone). Start with short intervals (e.g., 25 minutes) and gradually increase the duration as you build your focus muscle.

2. **Time boxing:** Allocate specific blocks of time to each task on your to-do list. This helps create a clear structure for your day and prevents tasks from expanding to fill the available time. Be realistic about how long each task will take and schedule short breaks between blocks of focused work.

3. **Batch Processing:** Group similar tasks together and complete them in batches. This can help minimize context switching and improve efficiency. For example, respond to emails in batches rather than checking your inbox constantly throughout the day.

4. **The "One Thing" Focus:** Identify the single most important task that will have the greatest impact on your goals. Start your day by tackling this task while your energy and focus are high. This ensures that you make progress on your most important priorities, even if distractions arise later in the day.

5. **Mindful Transitions:** When transitioning between tasks, take a few moments to pause, breathe deeply, and clear your mind. This helps you mentally reset and approach each new task with fresh focus. You can also use this time to reflect on what you have accomplished and what you plan to do next.

Chapter Three: Reclaiming Your Attention

The Myth of Multitasking: Why It Doesn't Work

In today's fast-paced, information-rich environment, the ability to multitask is frequently lauded as a useful skill, a badge of pride for people who can manage numerous activities at once. We take pride in our ability to answer emails while attending a conference, read through social media while watching TV, and make supper while talking on the phone. However, the idea that we can successfully multitask is a fallacy, reinforced by our culture's fixation with productivity and efficiency.

Scientific study has repeatedly demonstrated that our brains are not designed for true multitasking. When we strive to complete numerous tasks at once, we are not doing so simultaneously. Instead, our brains swiftly move between tasks, a phenomenon known as task switching. This frequent shifting of concentration comes at a cost, as our brains require time and mental energy to refocus on each job.

According to studies, task switching can have a considerable negative impact on performance and productivity. When we switch between tasks, we incur a cognitive cost because our brains must reorient themselves to the new activity. This can lead to blunders, delays, and a general feeling of mental fatigue. According to research, it might take up to 25 minutes to fully restore focus following an interruption.

Furthermore, task switching can impede our ability to think critically and creatively. Continuously switching tasks prevents us from fully engaging in any one. This can keep us from attaining a state of flow, in which we are completely involved in our task and capable of producing our finest work.

Multitasking reinforces the misconception by providing a sense of control. When we feel like we are juggling many tasks, we feel like we are getting more done when we are juggling many tasks. However, this sense is frequently deceptive. In reality, attempting to multitask typically results in less productivity because the constant shift of focus leads to inefficiencies and errors.

Instead of multitasking, we should concentrate on single-tasking, which means giving our undivided attention to one job at a time. By focusing on a single activity, we can achieve a state of flow in which we are completely absorbed in our job and can produce our finest work. This not only increases productivity, but it also improves our job happiness and enjoyment.

Of fact, in today's fast-paced environment, it is not always feasible to avoid multitasking entirely. However, there are ways we can reduce the negative impact of task switching while increasing productivity.

One such method is batching, which is grouping related tasks and performing them in a single block of time. Instead of monitoring your email all day, you might schedule specified times to respond to emails in batches. This can help limit the number of times you have to switch jobs, allowing you to devote more time to each one.

Another method is to prioritize your duties, focusing on the most critical first. This ensures that you continue to make progress toward your most important goals, even if you are distracted by other duties. By defining the most critical jobs for you,

you may prevent wasting time on things that can be completed later.

Additionally, it is critical to provide a distraction-free environment. This may include shutting off notifications, silencing your phone, and finding a quiet space to work. By reducing external distractions, you can generate the mental space required for profound concentration.

Finally, it is critical to develop mindfulness. Mindfulness is the practice of focusing on the present moment without judgment. By practicing mindfulness, we can become more aware of when our attention wanders and gently guide it back to the work in hand. This can help us maintain attention and avoid the hazards of multitasking.

The Power of Single-Tasking: Focusing on What Matters

Cal Newport, a computer science professor, developed the term "deep work," which refers to the ability to focus without distraction on a cognitively difficult activity. It's a state of flow in which we're completely engrossed in our task, and time seems to slip away. In this mood, we can do our best work, solve complex challenges, and generate new ideas.

Sustained focus, the foundation of serious work, is a muscle that needs to be trained and developed. In a world of continual notifications, emails, and social media updates, our attention spans have been reduced to mere seconds. However, by intentionally choosing to single-task, we can progressively improve our attention and recapture our ability to concentrate for long periods of time.

The advantages of prolonged focus are numerous. First and foremost, it greatly increases our productivity. When we are totally involved in a task, we may work more efficiently and effectively, accomplishing it in less time and with fewer mistakes. This not only saves time but also frees up brain resources for other vital tasks.

Furthermore, prolonged focus promotes creativity and invention. When we are fully engaged in a topic or project, our minds can establish connections and generate new ideas that would not be feasible if we were distracted. This is why so many discoveries and advancements have occurred during periods of quiet thought and intense focus.

Sustained focus has a significant impact on our wellbeing. When we are completely present in the moment, we are less likely to experience stress or overload. We are able to completely appreciate the task at hand and feel satisfied with our achievements. This can lead to a stronger sense of purpose and fulfillment in both our professional and personal lives.

So, how do we teach our brains to concentrate better and maintain continuous focus? The first step is to establish a distraction-free workplace. This includes turning off notifications, silencing our phones, and finding a quiet area where we can work uninterrupted. It also entails setting boundaries with others and informing them that we require uninterrupted time to focus.

Another critical stage is to cultivate mindfulness. Mindfulness is the practice of focusing on the present moment without judgment. By practicing mindfulness, we can become more aware of when our attention wanders and gently guide it back to the work in hand. This can be accomplished by simple activities like meditation, deep breathing, or simply pausing to examine our environment and thoughts.

Time management skills can also help us train our brains to concentrate more effectively. The Pomodoro Technique, for example, consists of working for 25 minutes and then taking a 5-minute rest. This systematic method can help us break down enormous activities into more manageable portions while avoiding burnout.

Furthermore, it is critical to prioritize our jobs and concentrate on the most important ones first. This assures that we are making progress toward our most important goals, even if we are distracted by other duties. By selecting the most critical jobs for us, we may prevent wasting time on work that can be completed later.

Self-Reflective Questions:

1. **Multitasking Habits:** In what areas of my life do I tend to multitask the most? What are the specific tasks or activities that I often try to combine? (Make a list or journal about your multitasking habits).

2. **Effectiveness of Multitasking:** When I multitask, do I feel like I am truly accomplishing more, or am I simply switching my attention back and forth between tasks? (Reflect on how multitasking impacts your overall productivity and quality of work).

3. **Attention Residue:** After switching between tasks, do I find it difficult to fully refocus on the new task? How long does it typically take for me to regain my concentration? (Observe how task switching affects your focus and concentration).

4. **Deep Work Potential:** What are the activities or projects in my life that would benefit most from deep, focused work? How can I create more opportunities for deep work in my schedule? (Identify tasks that require sustained attention and plan dedicated blocks of time for them).

5. **Value of Single-Tasking:** If I were to fully embrace single-tasking, how would it change my approach to work, my productivity levels, and my overall sense of well-being? (Imagine the positive impact that single-tasking could have on your life).

Transformative Exercises:

1. **Mono-Tasking Challenge:** Choose one important task and commit to completing it without any distractions. Turn off notifications, close unnecessary tabs, and focus solely on that task until it is finished. Observe how your focus and efficiency improve when you dedicate your full attention to a single activity.

2. **Task Switching Awareness:** Pay attention to how often you switch between tasks throughout the day. When you catch yourself task switching, pause and ask yourself: "Is this the most important thing I should be doing right now?" If not, refocus your attention on the task at hand.

3. **Mindful Transitions:** Practice mindful transitions between tasks. Before switching to a new activity, take a few deep breaths, clear your mind, and consciously shift your focus to the new task. This can help reduce attention residue and improve your overall concentration.

4. **Deep Work Ritual:** Create a ritual to help you transition into a state of deep work. This could

involve finding a quiet workspace, setting a timer, listening to calming music, or using a specific app or tool to block distractions. Experiment with different rituals to find what works best for you.

5. **Pomodoro Technique:** Implement the Pomodoro Technique to break down your work into focused intervals. Set a timer for 25 minutes and work on a single task without distractions. After each interval, take a 5-minute break. Repeat this cycle four times, then take a longer break of 20-30 minutes. This structured approach can help improve focus and prevent burnout.

Chapter Four: Setting Clear Goals

Defining Your Vision: Creating a Compelling Why

Defining our vision, unique purpose, and direction in life is the first step towards regaining our focus and living a meaningful and rewarding life.

Consider your vision to be a lighthouse that guides you across the stormy seas of distraction. It is the North Star that guides you and keeps you on track, even when temptation threatens to pull you off course. Without a clear vision, we risk drifting aimlessly, surrendering to the whims of the moment and the attraction of immediate fulfillment.

So, how do we define our vision? It all starts with a thorough dive into our beliefs, passions, and long-term goals. Values are guiding concepts that influence our decisions and actions. Our values define us and what we stand for. Spend some time reflecting on your values. What are the most essential aspects of your life? Is it truth, integrity, kindness, creativity, or something else? Once you've discovered your basic principles, think about how you can use these values in your daily life.

Passions are activities, interests, or causes that spark a fire within us. These are the activities we enjoy that make us feel alive and energized. What are you enthusiastic about? What causes your heart to sing? What activities help you lose yourself? When you are immersed in your passions, time seems to fly by, and you feel a profound feeling of delight and contentment.

Our dreams and goals for the future are long-term aspirations. These are the goals we hope to achieve and the influence we want to have on the world. What do you envision for your life in the coming years? What legacy do you hope to leave behind? What kind of person do you hope to become?

Once you have a better knowledge of your beliefs, passions, and goals, you can start articulating your vision. This can shape into a personal mission statement, a vision board, or simply a set of goals and intents. The main thing is to make a physical representation of your vision that you can refer to and be inspired by.

The process of defining your vision is not always simple. It demands insight, honesty, and bravery.

You may need to face difficult questions about your priorities, fears, and doubts. But the benefits of these processes are immeasurable. A clear vision can help you feel more purposeful, directed, and motivated. It can help you make better decisions, overcome obstacles, and stay focused on your goals despite distractions.

Developing a compelling "why" is an essential component of defining your vision. Your "why" is the reason behind your goals, the motivator that propels you forward. It is the answer to the question, "Why do I want to achieve this?" A strong "why" can motivate you and keep you focused on your vision even when things get tough.

To figure out "why," ask yourself the following questions:

- Why do I want to accomplish my goals?
- What impact do I want to have on the world?
- What kind of person do I hope to become?
- What legacy do I hope to leave behind?

The answers to these questions will assist you in determining the deeper meaning of your goals and developing a "why" that is both personal and powerful.

In a world that constantly pulls us in different directions, a clear vision is a powerful distraction-reduction tool. It provides us with a sense of purpose and direction, allowing us to focus our energy and attention on the things that truly matter. By taking the time to define your vision and create a compelling "why," you can unlock your full potential and achieve your most ambitious goals.

SMART Goals: Setting Yourself Up for Success

In a world when our attention is continually drawn in a million different directions, creating clear, actionable goals is more crucial than ever. It's not enough to have a vague concept of what you want to accomplish; you need a roadmap, a clear plan to guide you through the inevitable distractions and roadblocks. Here's where the SMART goal structure comes in. SMART is an acronym for Specific, Measurable, Achievable, Relevant, and Time-bound. By incorporating this framework into your goal-setting process, you can turn your dreams into tangible activities, paving the road for focused growth and, ultimately, success.

Let us break down each component of the SMART framework.

- **Specific**: Make sure your goals are clear and well-defined. Avoid using imprecise statements such as "I want to be healthier" or "I want to be more successful." Instead, be explicit about what you hope to achieve. Instead of expressing "I

want to be healthier," you may say "I want to lose 10 pounds in three months by exercising three times per week and eating a well-balanced diet."
- **Measurable**: You can track your progress and know when you've met your goals if they're measurable. Instead of expressing "I want to read more," try saying, "I want to read one book per month." Setting quantifiable goals provides a clear target to aim for and allows you to readily evaluate your progress along the way.
- **Achievable**: Your objectives should be practical and achievable. While it is beneficial to aim large, adopting unreasonable goals might result in disappointment and despair. Instead, make goals that are challenging but still achievable. When defining goals, take into account your resources, talents, and time limits.
- **Relevant**: Your goals should be in line with your values and priorities. Ask yourself why this objective is essential to you and how it will help you achieve your overall life vision. Setting meaningful goals ensures that your efforts are focused on the things that are actually important to you.
- **Time-bound**: Set a deadline for your goals. This provides a sense of urgency and keeps you on track. Instead of expressing "I want to learn a new language," try saying "I want to be conversational in Spanish by the end of the year." Setting a deadline provides you with a timeline within which to work and allows you to break

down your objective into smaller, more doable steps.

The SMART goal framework is more than simply a collection of instructions; it's an effective tool for changing the way you approach your goals. Using this structure, you may transform your dreams into actionable strategies, boosting your chances of success and reducing the risk of becoming sidetracked by distractions.

Let us provide an example to demonstrate how the SMART framework can be utilized. Assume your goal is to enhance your fitness. Instead of saying "I want to get in shape," a SMART goal would be: "I want to run a 5K race in under 30 minutes within six months by following a training plan and running three times a week." This objective is explicit (ran a 5K race in less than 30 minutes), measurable (with correct training), relevant (aligned with the desire to improve fitness), and time-bound (within six months).

Setting a SMART objective like this provides a clear path to follow. You understand what you need to do (follow a training plan and run three times per week), how to track your progress (track your running time), and when you need to reach your objective. This clarity and focus may be extremely inspiring, particularly in a world filled with distractions.

It is crucial to remember that SMART goals are not set in stone. They can be modified and refined as necessary.

Life is unpredictable, and circumstances may change. If you discover that a goal is no longer relevant or attainable, do not be afraid to alter it. The goal is to be flexible and adaptive while still having a clear sense of direction.

In addition to defining smart goals, it is critical to monitor your progress. This can be accomplished through a variety of approaches, including writing, utilizing goal-tracking software, or simply checking in with oneself on a regular basis. Tracking your progress allows you to celebrate your triumphs, discover areas for improvement, and stay inspired as you work toward your goals.

Self-Reflective Questions:

1. **Goal Clarity:** Are my current goals specific and well-defined, or are they vague and open-ended? Can I clearly articulate what I want to achieve, or do my goals need more refinement? (This is a good opportunity to write down your current goals and assess their clarity).

2. **Measurable Milestones:** How will I measure my progress towards my goals? What specific metrics or indicators will I use to track my success? (Identify quantifiable milestones for each goal to make progress tangible).

3. **Achievability Assessment:** Are my goals realistic and attainable given my current resources, skills, and time constraints? Am I

setting myself up for success or disappointment? (Be honest with yourself about the feasibility of your goals and adjust them if necessary).

4. **Relevance Check:** Are my goals aligned with my values, passions, and overall vision for my life? Do they contribute to my personal growth and fulfillment, or are they driven by external pressures or expectations? (Reflect on the deeper "why" behind your goals).

5. **Time-Bound Commitment:** Have I set clear deadlines for my goals? Do I have a timeline in place to ensure that I am making consistent progress and staying on track? (Create a timeline or action plan for each goal with specific milestones and deadlines).

Transformative Exercises:

1. **Goal Visualization:** Spend a few minutes each day visualizing yourself achieving your goals. Imagine the sights, sounds, feelings, and emotions associated with reaching your desired outcomes. This practice can help strengthen your motivation and commitment.

2. **SMART Goal Refinement:** Take your existing goals and refine them using the SMART criteria (Specific, Measurable, Achievable, Relevant, Time-Bound). Rewrite each goal in a clear, concise, and actionable format.

3. **Vision Board Creation:** Create a vision board (physical or digital) to visually represent your goals. Collect images, quotes, and words that inspire you and reflect your aspirations. Display your vision board in a prominent place where you will see it regularly as a reminder of your goals.

4. **Accountability Partner:** Share your goals with a trusted friend, family member, or mentor who can serve as an accountability partner. Regular check-ins with your accountability partner can help you stay motivated and on track.

5. **Goal Review Ritual:** Set aside time each week or month to review your goals and assess your progress. Celebrate your successes, identify any obstacles or challenges, and adjust your plan as needed. This regular review process helps you stay focused and adaptable.

Chapter Five: Prioritizing with Purpose

The Eisenhower Matrix: Urgent vs. Important

The Eisenhower Matrix, a simple but effective technique credited to President Dwight D. Eisenhower, provides a framework for distinguishing the truly important from the merely urgent, allowing us to make intentional decisions about how we spend our time and energy. Understanding and following the ideas of this matrix allows us to cut through the noise, focus on what is genuinely important, and make significant progress toward our goals.

The Eisenhower Matrix is a two-by-two grid that assigns jobs according to their urgency and importance. The vertical axis denotes importance, with "Important" at the top and "Not Important" at the bottom. The horizontal axis denotes urgency, with "Urgent" on the left and "Not Urgent" on the right. This results in four separate quadrants, each having its own consequences for how we should approach the tasks within them.

The first quadrant, Urgent and Important, is where crises and pressing deadlines exist. These are the chores that require our immediate attention and cannot be overlooked without consequences. Examples include reacting to an urgent client request, completing a vital deadline, or dealing with a family emergency. While these duties are clearly vital, it is critical to note that devoting too much time to this sector might result in a reactive and stressful lifestyle. The goal is to reduce the quantity of tasks in this quadrant by prioritizing important tasks before they become urgent.

The second quadrant, Important but Not Urgent, represents prospects for growth, development, and long-term success. These are the chores that help us achieve our goals and values but do not have an urgent deadline. Examples include future planning, acquiring a new skill, exercising, and cultivating relationships. This quadrant is where we may have the greatest impact on our lives, yet it is also the most readily overlooked in the face of pressing needs. Prioritizing chores in this quadrant allows us to invest in our future and live a more satisfying and balanced life.

The third quadrant, Urgent but Not Important, is where distractions and interruptions frequently occur. These are the chores that require our attention but do not advance our aims or values. Examples include responding to irrelevant emails, attending ineffective meetings, and scrolling through social media. While these duties may appear urgent in the moment, they can lead to a cycle of busywork that diverts our attention away from our genuine objectives. By learning to detect and avoid these distractions, we can free up our time and energy for more worthwhile activities.

The fourth quadrant, Not Urgent and Not Important, contains time-wasting and inconsequential tasks. These are the jobs that don't add to our aims or require our immediate attention. Examples include watching television, playing video games, and gossiping. While these activities can be enjoyable in moderation, spending too much time in this sector can leave you feeling empty and unfulfilled. By reducing our time in this area, we can make room for more meaningful and fulfilling experiences.

The Eisenhower Matrix is more than simply a theoretical framework; it's a useful tool for our daily lives. By dividing our work into these four quadrants, we may make better decisions about how to spend our time and effort. We can prioritise key tasks, delegate or remove those that are unimportant, and take a more focused and intentional approach to our professional and personal life.

To use the Eisenhower Matrix efficiently, first make a list of all the tasks that need to be completed. Then, assess each task's urgency and relevance and allocate it to the proper quadrant. Once you've categorized your jobs, you can start prioritizing them, beginning with the Urgent and Important quadrant and on to the Important but Not Urgent quadrant. Tasks in the Urgent but Not Important quadrant can frequently be assigned or deleted, whilst those in the Not Urgent and Not Important quadrant should be reduced or avoided entirely.

The Pareto Principle: The 80/20 Rule of Productivity

A principle that could help us cut through the noise and focus on the most important tasks? What if we could accomplish more while doing less? Enter the Pareto Principle, a strong notion that has the potential to transform how we approach productivity and goal achievement in today's distracted environment.

The Pareto Principle, commonly known as the 80/20 rule, posits that approximately 80% of outcomes result from 20% of causes. This idea, discovered by Italian economist Vilfredo Pareto in the late nineteenth century, has subsequently been applied to a variety of sectors, including business and economics, personal productivity, and time management. In essence, the Pareto Principle states that a small number of inputs or actions account for a disproportionately large share of the outcomes.

When it comes to productivity, the Pareto Principle states that 80% of our results come from 20% of our labor. This suggests that a small number of tasks account for the majority of our accomplishments, with the remaining 80% contributing just significantly to our overall success. Identifying and focusing on these high-impact jobs allows us to do more with less effort, freeing up time and energy for other critical aspects of our lives.

So, how can we determine which 20% of tasks produce 80% of the results? The first stage is to record your time and activities for a week or two. This will offer you a clear view of how you are currently allocating your time and which chores are taking up the majority of your day. Once you have this information, you may begin analyzing it and identifying trends.

Look for projects that routinely yield big outcomes or help you get closer to your goals. These are probably the high-impact tasks you should prioritize. Think about the tasks you enjoy or that match your skills and interests. These tasks are likely to be more rewarding and stimulating, resulting in increased productivity and pleasure.

Once you've discovered your high-impact tasks, begin prioritizing them. This entails blocking off time on your schedule for these chores and keeping it free of distractions. It also involves being willing to say "no" to less important duties or obligations that may be transferred to others.

Applying the Pareto Principle in your daily life can result in considerable increases in productivity, focus, and overall well-being. Focusing on the activities that genuinely matter allows you to do more with less effort, freeing up time and energy for other vital aspects of your life. You can also reduce stress and overwhelm by not attempting to do everything.

The Pareto Principle can be used to prioritize tasks as well as other aspects of your life. In your relationships, focus on the few people who bring you the most joy and contentment. You can also use it to manage your finances, focusing on the few investments that yield the highest returns.

The Pareto Principle is a useful tool for cutting through the noise and focusing on what truly matters. Identifying and prioritizing your high-impact tasks allows you to do more with less effort, minimize stress, and live a more fulfilling life.

Self-Reflective Questions:

1. **Goal Clarity:** Are my current goals specific and well-defined, or are they vague and open-ended? Can I clearly articulate what I want to achieve, or do my goals need more refinement? (This is a good opportunity to write down your current goals and assess their clarity).
2. **Measurable Milestones:** How will I measure my progress towards my goals? What specific metrics or indicators will I use to track my success? (Identify quantifiable milestones for each goal to make progress tangible).
3. **Achievability Assessment:** Are my goals realistic and attainable given my current resources, skills, and time constraints? Am I setting myself up for success or disappointment? (Be honest with yourself about the feasibility of your goals and adjust them if necessary).
4. **Relevance Check:** Are my goals aligned with my values, passions, and overall vision for my life? Do they contribute to my personal growth and fulfillment, or are they driven by external pressures or expectations? (Reflect on the deeper "why" behind your goals).
5. **Time-Bound Commitment:** Have I set clear deadlines for my goals? Do I have a timeline in place to ensure that I am making consistent progress and staying on track?

(Create a timeline or action plan for each goal with specific milestones and deadlines).

Transformative Exercises:

1. **Goal Visualization:** Spend a few minutes each day visualizing yourself achieving your goals. Imagine the sights, sounds, feelings, and emotions associated with reaching your desired outcomes. This practice can help strengthen your motivation and commitment.
2. **SMART Goal Refinement:** Take your existing goals and refine them using the SMART criteria (Specific, Measurable, Achievable, Relevant, Time-Bound). Rewrite each goal in a clear, concise, and actionable format.
3. **Vision Board Creation:** Create a vision board (physical or digital) to visually represent your goals. Collect images, quotes, and words that inspire you and reflect your aspirations. Display your vision board in a prominent place where you will see it regularly as a reminder of your goals.
4. **Accountability Partner:** Share your goals with a trusted friend, family member, or mentor who can serve as an accountability partner. Regular check-ins with your accountability partner can help you stay motivated and on track.
5. **Goal Review Ritual:** Set aside time each week or month to review your goals and

assess your progress. Celebrate your successes, identify any obstacles or challenges, and adjust your plan as needed. This regular review process helps you stay focused and adaptable.

Chapter Six: Time Management Techniques:

The Pomodoro Technique: Working with Time, Not Against It

In the battle for attention and productivity, a simple yet powerful strategy has emerged as a light of hope for people who struggle to stay on target in today's distracting world. The Pomodoro Technique, named after the tomato-shaped kitchen timer employed by its developer, Francesco Cirillo, is an organized approach to time management that has the potential to revolutionize how we work and learn.

At its essence, the Pomodoro Technique is elegantly simple. It entails dividing your work into 25-minute intervals known as "pomodoros," followed by brief 5-minute breaks. After four pomodoros, take a 20-

30-minute pause. This cycle of focused work followed by short pauses establishes a routine that helps to retain energy and prevent burnout.

The Pomodoro technique's beauty lies in its ability to harness the power of focused attention. During each pomodoro, you commit to completing a single activity without interruptions. This means no reading emails, no surfing through social media, and no answering the phone—simply complete focus on the task at hand. This concentrated effort enables you to achieve a state of flow, in which you are completely involved in your job and able to make excellent progress.

The short intervals that occur after each pomodoro are equally important. They offer a chance to rest and refresh, both emotionally and physically. Taking a break from your job, even for a few minutes, can help you clear your mind, reduce eye strain, and avoid mental tiredness. This can result in increased creativity, better problem-solving abilities, and a higher sense of well-being.

One of the most significant advantages of the Pomodoro Technique is its ability to divide enormous, scary jobs into smaller, more manageable parts. This can make even the most complex jobs seem less daunting and more manageable. Focusing on one 25-minute increment at a time allows you to make consistent progress without feeling overwhelmed.

The strategy also encourages you to be more intentional with your job. Before each pomodoro, you determine which task you will focus on and estimate how many pomodoros it will take to finish. This allows you to prioritize your tasks and better manage your time. Furthermore, by measuring your pomodoros, you can gain valuable insights into your work routines and identify areas for efficiency improvement.

While the traditional 25-minute work/5-minute break cycle is effective for many people, the Pomodoro Technique is very adaptable. You can customize the length of your pomodoros and breaks to meet your own needs and work style. Some people find that longer pomodoros (e.g., 50 minutes) are more successful for jobs that require intense concentration, whereas others prefer shorter pomodoros (e.g., 10 minutes) for more repetitive or less taxing work.

The trick is to experiment and discover a rhythm that suits you. If you find it difficult to focus for 25 minutes, consider cutting your pomodoros to 15 or 20 minutes. If you find yourself becoming restless during your breaks, consider taking a longer break or indulging in a new activity, such as going for a walk or listening to music.

The Pomodoro Technique is more than simply a time management technique; it is a mental revolution. It helps you be more careful with your time and attention, work more deliberately, and take breaks when needed. Implementing this strategy may help you regain your attention, increase your productivity, and achieve your goals in a distracted environment.

The Pomodoro Technique can help you be more productive in your daily life, whether you are a student striving to study for exams, a professional trying to meet deadlines, or just someone who wants to be more efficient. It's a simple yet powerful technique to avoid distractions, enhance attention, and reach your maximum potential.

Time Blocking: Scheduling Your Day for Maximum Focus

Time blocking is the process of partitioning your day into discrete blocks of time, each allocated to a specific job or set of chores. Instead of just making a to-do list and hoping to tackle each item as time allows, time blocking involves assigning a set time slot to each job, essentially creating a timetable for the day.

This systematic approach to time management provides numerous key advantages. First and foremost, it helps to reduce context switching, which is the mental effort necessary to change our attention from one task to another. When we switch between occupations during the day, our brains are continuously reorienting themselves, which can contribute to mental tiredness and lower productivity. By allocating distinct blocks of time to each activity, we may limit the amount of context switching and concentrate more deeply on the work at hand.

Second, time restriction helps us prioritize our most critical duties. By giving specific time slots to our high-priority jobs, we ensure that they receive the attention they require. This keeps us from becoming bogged down in unimportant duties or succumbing to the tyranny of the urgent.

Third, time blocking can help us establish a sense of organization and control in our lives. When we have a set routine for the day, we are less likely to feel overwhelmed or worried. Being aware of what to do and when may help us stay calm and focused.

So, how do you use time blocks in your own life? The first step is to determine your most important duties. These tasks will most affect your goals and priorities. Once you've selected these tasks, you can start scheduling precise blocks of time for them in your calendar.

The length of each time block varies depending on the nature of the assignment. For things that demand intense focus, such as writing or complicated problem solving, you may want to set aside longer periods of time, such as 90 minutes or two hours. For less taxing chores, such as reading email or returning phone calls, consider allocating shorter blocks of time, such as 30 minutes or an hour.

When planning your time blocks, be realistic about how long each task will take. It's also a beneficial idea to leave some buffer time between jobs to account for any unexpected disruptions or delays.

Once you've established your time blocks, it's critical to stick to them as much as possible. This entails avoiding distractions and interruptions throughout your focused work hours. You may wish to disable notifications on your phone and computer, close your email inbox, and find a quiet spot to work.

Of course, there will be occasions when unforeseen events occur that force you to change your timetable. However, if you have a clear plan in place, you will be better prepared to deal with these disruptions and get back on track faster.

Time limiting isn't a one-size-fits-all solution. The best approach to using this strategy is to experiment and see what works best for you. Some people prefer to make a comprehensive itinerary for their entire day, but others prefer to set aside time for their most critical chores while leaving the rest of their day open.

The goal is to establish a system that works for you and can be followed consistently. With practice, time blocking can become an effective technique for increasing productivity, lowering stress, and attaining your objectives in a distracted world.

Self-Reflective Questions:

1. **Time Awareness:** How accurate is my perception of time? Do I tend to overestimate or underestimate how long tasks will take? (Consider tracking your time for a day to compare your estimates with reality).
2. **Current Techniques:** What time management techniques am I currently using, if any? Are they effective in helping me stay focused and productive? (Reflect on your current strategies and their impact on your time management).
3. **Peak Performance:** When do I feel most energized and focused during the day? How can I schedule my most important tasks during these peak performance times? (Identify your peak hours and align your schedule accordingly).
4. **Procrastination Patterns:** What are my typical procrastination triggers? What excuses do I tell myself to avoid starting or completing tasks? (Become aware of your procrastination patterns and identify strategies to overcome them).

5. **Flexibility vs. Rigidity:** Am I too rigid in my scheduling, or do I allow for flexibility and adaptability? How can I strike a balance between structure and spontaneity in my time management approach? (Reflect on your need for both structure and flexibility to create a sustainable time management system).

Transformative Exercises:

1. **Pomodoro Practice:** Commit to using the Pomodoro Technique for a week. Set a timer for 25 minutes, focus on a single task without distractions, and take a 5-minute break. Repeat this cycle four times, then take a longer break of 20-30 minutes. Observe how this structured approach impacts your focus and productivity.
2. **Timeboxing Experiment:** Try timeboxing your tasks for a day. Assign specific time slots to each task on your to-do list and commit to working on that task only during its allocated time. Notice how this helps you prioritize and avoid overcommitting to any single activity.
3. **Energy Management:** Instead of solely focusing on time management, pay attention to your energy levels throughout the day. Schedule demanding tasks when you are most alert and energized, and schedule less mentally taxing tasks for times when your energy dips.

4. **Time Tracking Challenge:** Track your time for a few days to gain insights into how you are spending your hours. This can be done using a time-tracking app or simply jotting down your activities. Once you have a clear picture of your time usage, identify areas where you can make adjustments to optimize your productivity.
5. **Procrastination Buster:** Choose a task that you have been procrastinating on and break it down into smaller, more manageable steps. Commit to completing the first step today and set a deadline for each subsequent step. This can help you overcome inertia and gain momentum.

Chapter Seven: Designing Your Workspace

Decluttering: Creating a Calm and Organized Space

In our persistent quest for productivity and focus, we frequently ignore the enormous influence our surroundings have on our capacity to concentrate and achieve our objectives. The surroundings we inhabit, both physical and digital, can either help us focus or become breeding grounds for distractions. A messy desk, an overflowing email, or a disorderly digital workspace may all subtly undercut our efforts by diverting our attention in a variety of places, leaving us feeling overwhelmed and distracted. But what if there was a way to create a haven of peace and clarity in the middle of chaos? What if we could declutter our surroundings, both literally and digitally, to create an environment that encourages focus, creativity, and relaxation?

Decluttering is the practice of letting go. It is about discovering and removing concrete and intangible objects from our lives that are no longer useful to us. This approach can be both freeing and empowering because it frees up physical and mental space for what really matters.

Let us start with our physical spaces. Our homes, businesses, and workspaces should be places of calm, not tension and distraction. A crowded desk, piled high with papers, knick-knacks, and other random stuff, can create a visual disarray that makes it difficult to focus. Similarly, a chaotic home with piles of clothes, books, and other items can make us feel overwhelmed and difficult to relax.

To simplify your physical area, begin by evaluating which items you use frequently and which you do not. Be honest with yourself about what you need and can let go. Ask yourself questions like, "Do I use this item frequently?" "Does it bring me joy or add value to my life?" "Could someone else benefit from this item more than I do?"

After choosing items to get rid of, act. Donate or sell items in excellent shape, recycle or dispose of items that are no longer useful, and designate a space for whatever you wish to preserve. The idea is to design a room that is both useful and aesthetically beautiful, allowing you to breathe deeply and concentrate on your work or other interests.

Decluttering your digital space is equally vital as decluttering your physical space. In today's digital age, our computers, cell phones, and other devices have become storage hubs for massive amounts of data. Emails, documents, images, movies, and other digital items may soon pile up, resulting in a virtual wasteland that is just as irritating as a cluttered workstation.

To declutter your digital environment, first organize your files and folders. Create a clear and logical method for storing your documents so that you can discover what you're looking for quickly. Delete or archive unnecessary emails, unsubscribe from newsletters and mailing lists, and organize your photographs and videos into albums or folders.

Also, know what apps and programs you use on your devices. Do you really need all of those social media, news, and gaming apps? If not, consider removing or disabling them in order to reduce distractions and regain focus.

Creating a minimalist home does not imply getting rid of all you own or adopting an ascetic lifestyle. Being intentional about what you acquire and making sure it has meaning is key. It is about establishing an environment in which you can breathe, think, and create without being distracted.

By decluttering your physical and digital surroundings, you may create a sanctuary of quiet and clarity that will help you focus and be more productive. A clean and well-organized environment can help you relax, concentrate better, and be more creative. It can also provide a sensation of calm and relaxation, allowing you to refresh and regenerate.

Ergonomics: Optimizing Your Physical Environment

The way we sit, the lighting we utilize, the height of our desks, and even the temperature of our office can all have a big impact on our comfort and, ultimately, our cognitive performance. In a world full of distractions, designing an ergonomic workstation is more than just about comfort; it's a deliberate investment in our capacity to focus and achieve our goals.

Ergonomics, the study of designing workspaces to fit the human body, is frequently dismissed as a specialized concern for people who have pre-existing physical conditions. However, its concepts are useful for everyone looking to improve their performance and well-being. By designing our workspaces to meet our physiological needs, we may reduce physical strain, avoid discomfort and injury, and foster sustained focus and productivity.

Let us begin with the desk, which is the foundation of any workspace. Your desk's height has a significant impact on your posture and comfort throughout the day. A workstation that is too high or too low might result in bent shoulders, strained necks, and sore backs. Ideally, your desk should be set at a height that allows your forearms to rest comfortably on the surface, elbows bent at a 90-degree angle. This neutral posture reduces tension on your muscles and joints, allowing you to work longer without discomfort.

Your chair is another important aspect of an ergonomic workplace. A decent chair should give enough back support, encourage proper posture, and allow you to modify the seat height and backrest angle to suit your needs. Look for a chair with lumbar support to retain your spine's natural curve and adjustable armrests to keep your shoulders comfortable.

Lighting is frequently underestimated, although it plays a critical part in our ability to concentrate and minimize eye strain. Bright fluorescent lighting can be tiring and induce headaches, while low lighting can make it difficult to see properly and create eye strain. Ideally, your office should contain a mix of natural and artificial lighting. If feasible, place your desk near a window to benefit from natural light, which has been found to boost mood and productivity. Adjustable task lighting can supplement natural light by directing it where it is most needed.

Temperature also affects our comfort and focus. A workspace that is too hot or too cold can be distracting and difficult to concentrate in. Most people believe that a temperature of 68 to 72 degrees Fahrenheit is ideal for productivity. If you can't manage the temperature in your entire workstation, try utilizing a personal fan or heater to create a comfortable microclimate around your desk.

In addition to these fundamental ergonomic concepts, there are additional elements to consider while creating your workspace. For example, the position of your computer monitor is critical in decreasing eye strain and neck pain. Your monitor should be placed squarely in front of you, about an arm's length away, with the top of the screen at or slightly below eye level.

Positioning your keyboard and mouse is also critical for avoiding wrist pain and carpal tunnel syndrome. Your keyboard should be positioned with your wrists straight and your forearms parallel to the floor. To use your mouse without straining, make it easy to reach.

Finally, you should take regular breaks to stretch and move around. Sitting for lengthy periods of time might be detrimental for our health, so we should get up and move about every 20-30 minutes. A quick walk around the office or a few simple stretches can help increase circulation, relieve muscle tension, and clear your thoughts.

Self-Reflective Questions:

1. **Workspace Assessment:** How does my current workspace make me feel? Does it promote focus and productivity, or does it leave me feeling distracted and overwhelmed? (Take a moment to observe your workspace and note your emotional response).
2. **Ergonomic Evaluation:** Is my workspace ergonomically designed? Does my desk, chair, and computer setup support good posture and physical comfort? (Consider whether your current setup could be contributing to any physical discomfort or pain).
3. **Clutter Inventory:** How much clutter do I have in my workspace? Is it filled with unnecessary items that are distracting or taking up valuable space? (Take an inventory of your workspace and identify items that could be removed or relocated).

4. **Sensory Influences:** How do the lighting, temperature, and noise levels in my workspace affect my focus and concentration? Are there any sensory elements that could be adjusted to create a more conducive environment? (Pay attention to how your senses are being stimulated in your workspace).
5. **Personalization:** Does my workspace reflect my personality and interests? Is it a space where I feel inspired and motivated to work? (Consider adding personal touches, such as plants, artwork, or meaningful objects, to create a more inviting and personalized workspace).

Transformative Exercises:

1. **Declutter Challenge:** Set a timer for 15 minutes and declutter your workspace. Remove any unnecessary items, organize your papers and files, and wipe down your desk. Notice how this simple act of tidying can create a sense of calm and clarity.
2. **Ergonomic Adjustment:** Experiment with adjusting the height of your desk, chair, and computer monitor to find an ergonomic setup that feels comfortable and supportive. Invest in ergonomic accessories, such as a keyboard wrist rest or a standing desk converter, if needed.
3. **Lighting Optimization:** Experiment with different lighting options in your workspace.

If possible, position your desk near a window to take advantage of natural light. Supplement natural light with adjustable task lighting to reduce eye strain and create a more inviting atmosphere.
4. **Sensory Exploration:** Pay attention to the sensory elements in your workspace and make adjustments as needed. If you are sensitive to noise, consider using noise-canceling headphones or listening to calming music. If you find certain scents relaxing, try using essential oils or scented candles to create a more pleasant environment.
5. **Workspace Makeover:** If your budget allows, consider a workspace makeover. Invest in a new desk, chair, or other ergonomic furniture. Add plants, artwork, or other personal touches to create a space that inspires and motivates you.

Chapter Eight: Minimizing Digital Distractions

Notifications Off: Taming the Digital Beast

In today's hyper connected world, notifications are ubiquitous, calling for our attention at every turn. Our phones constantly buzz, beep, and flash with alerts, ranging from social media updates and news headlines to email notifications and calendar reminders. While notifications can help us stay informed and connected, they can also be a big source of distraction, disrupting our focus and derailing our productivity.

Taming the digital beast of alerts is an important step in reclaiming our focus and achieving our goals. We can create a space favorable to concentration and intense work by gaining control of our digital surroundings and establishing technological limits.

The first step in recovering our attention is to disable non-essential notifications. While certain notifications, such as calendar reminders or urgent messages, may be useful, many are mere distractions that can be ignored. Social media updates, news alerts, and advertising emails can all be turned off without any serious effects.

Please check your phone and other notifications. Consider the question, "Does this notification truly require my immediate attention?" "Can this wait until later?" If the answer is no, simply turn it off. By deleting unwanted notifications, you may drastically limit the number of distractions you face throughout the day.

Another useful method is to set "Do Not Disturb" hours. This entails scheduling specified periods during the day when your phone and other gadgets stay silent and notifications are turned off. These hours can be spent for intense work, creative projects, or simply to relax.

To reduce distractions during your "Do Not Disturb" hours, turn off your phone's data connection or Wi-Fi. This stops incoming emails and notifications from disrupting your workflow. By scheduling these concentrated periods of time, you may educate your brain to enter a state of deep work and make outstanding progress on your most critical tasks.

In addition to disabling notifications and setting "Do Not Disturb" times, you may utilize app blockers to further limit your access to distracting apps and websites. These tools enable you to set time limitations for individual apps or completely prohibit them during certain hours of the day. For example, you may disable social media apps during work hours or limit your time spent on news websites to 30 minutes every day.

Using app blockers, you may build a digital environment that promotes focus and productivity. You can also use these tools to change undesirable habits, such as constantly checking your phone or skimming through social media feeds.

While turning off notifications, setting "Do Not Disturb" hours, and utilizing app blockers can help reduce distractions, keep in mind that they are only tools. Use these tools intentionally and find a balance that works for you.

For example, you may not want to disable all notifications because some may be necessary for your business or personal life. Instead, you may tailor your notification settings to only receive notifications from the most important apps and services.

Similarly, you may not want to set "Do Not Disturb" hours for the entire day, as this may render you unavailable to family, friends, or coworkers. Instead, schedule certain periods for serious work and take pauses throughout the day to check messages and react to emails.

Ultimately, the idea is to create a digital environment that encourages focus and productivity while also keeping you connected and informed. In a distracted environment, you can recover your attention and accomplish your goals by being careful of how you use technology and setting limits with your devices.

App Management: Curating Your Digital Tools

App management is the process of curating our digital tools, cleaning our gadgets, and organizing our apps in a way that aligns with our goals and priorities. It's about being conscious of the apps we use and ensuring that they serve us, not the other way around. Taking control of our digital space allows us to cultivate a more conscious relationship with our devices and recapture our focus in a distracted society.

The first step in app management is decluttering your devices. Begin by reviewing your home screen and app library. Ask yourself, "Do I really need this app?" "How often do I use it?" "Does it add value to my life?" Answering no to any of these questions suggests deleting the app. Be harsh in your review, and don't be afraid to delete apps you rarely use or that no longer serve a role in your life.

After you've decluttered your devices, sort the remaining apps into folders for specialized tasks. This allows you to quickly and easily access the programs you need without having to scroll through a cluttered homescreen. For example, you may make folders for "productivity," "social media," "news," "entertainment," and "utilities."

Think about your usage habits and priorities when organizing your apps into folders. Place the apps you use the most on your home screen or dock for quick access. Less commonly used apps can be organized into folders or on secondary displays. This lets you prioritize your favorite apps and save time finding them.

Another useful app management technique is to be aware of your app permissions. Many apps ask for access to your location, contacts, microphone, camera, and other sensitive information. Certain permissions are necessary for the program to work, while others are unnecessary or intrusive.

Check the permissions your apps request and disable any you don't want. This can help preserve your privacy and security while also limiting the amount of information that apps collect about you.

In addition to simplifying and organizing your apps, you can utilize app management tools to further personalize your digital experience. Many smartphones and tablets have features that allow you to set time limits for individual apps, track your app usage, and even block apps completely at certain times of day. These tools can help you reduce distractions and use your gadgets in a way that aligns with your objectives and priorities.

For example, you could limit the amount of time you spend looking through social media feeds. You may also measure your app usage to see how much time you spend on each app and where you might cut back. If you feel that certain apps are extremely distracting, you can disable them entirely during work hours or other times when you need to concentrate.

Taking control of your app management allows you to build a digital environment that promotes attention and productivity. You can also minimize distractions, preserve your privacy, and use your devices in a way that is consistent with your values and aspirations.

Remember that app management is an ongoing activity. As you download new apps or your priorities shift, you may need to reevaluate your app usage and make changes to your organizational scheme.

Self-Reflective Questions:

1. **Notification Overload:** How many notifications do I receive on an average day? Which ones are truly essential, and which ones are merely distractions? (Take an inventory of your notifications and categorize them based on their importance).
2. **Digital Habits:** How often do I check my phone or other devices throughout the day? Am I constantly refreshing social media feeds or checking for new emails, even when I'm not expecting anything important? (Reflect on your digital habits and how they may be affecting your focus).
3. **Screen Time:** How much time do I spend each day looking at screens? Is this amount of screen time aligned with my goals and priorities, or is it excessive and detrimental to my well-being? (Track your screen time for a week to gain insights into your digital usage patterns).
4. **FOMO (Fear of Missing Out):** Do I feel anxious or stressed when I'm not connected to my devices or social media? Do I feel like I'm missing out on important information or social interactions? (Reflect on your relationship with FOMO and how it may be driving your digital habits).

5. **Digital Boundaries:** Have I set any boundaries with my digital devices? Do I have specific times or places where I disconnect from technology and focus on other activities? (Consider whether you need to establish clearer boundaries with your devices to protect your focus and well-being).

Transformative Exercises:

1. **Notification Cleanse:** Go through your notification settings on your phone and other devices. Disable notifications for non-essential apps and services, and customize the notifications for essential apps to be less intrusive (e.g., no sounds or vibrations).
2. **Do Not Disturb Mode:** Experiment with using Do Not Disturb mode on your phone during specific times of the day, such as work hours, study sessions, or family time. This can help create distraction-free zones where you can focus without interruption.
3. **App Time Limits:** Set time limits for specific apps that you find particularly distracting, such as social media or games. Many devices and app stores offer built-in tools for setting time limits or you can use third-party apps to help you manage your app usage.
4. **Digital Detox:** Plan a regular digital detox where you disconnect from all digital devices for a set period. This could be for a few hours, a day, or even a weekend. Use this

time to engage in offline activities, connect with loved ones, or simply relax and recharge.
5. **Mindful Tech Use:** Practice mindful technology use by setting intentions before you engage with your devices. Ask yourself, "What am I trying to accomplish?" "How much time am I willing to spend on this activity?" Take regular breaks from screens throughout the day to rest your eyes and mind.

Chapter Nine: The Power of Habits

The Habit Loop: Understanding How Habits Work

In our never-ending search for personal growth and transformation, we frequently find ourselves struggling with deeply rooted behaviors that prevent us from attaining our true potential. These behaviors, whether it's idly scrolling through social media, delaying crucial work, or succumbing to unhealthy desires, can feel like insurmountable barriers to success. But what if we could understand the root causes of these patterns and rewire our brains for positive change?

Enter the habit loop, a powerful paradigm that reveals how habits are developed, maintained, and eventually modified. At its foundation, the habit loop is made up of three fundamental components:

the cue, routine, and reward. The cue is the stimulus that initiates the habit. It could be an external stimulus, such as a phone notification, or an interior state, like worry or boredom. The routine is the behavior itself—the set of activities you perform automatically in response to a stimulus. The reward is the positive consequence or emotion you experience as a result of your routine. This reward reinforces the habit, increasing the likelihood that you will repeat the activity in the future.

Understanding the habit loop is critical for overcoming undesired habits. Identifying the indicators that trigger our behaviors allows us to become more aware of when we are most likely to go back into previous routines. For example, if you find yourself compulsively reaching for your phone whenever you are bored, using boredom as a cue can help you break the habit loop before it starts.

Once we've recognized our cues, we can start modifying our routines. Instead of automatically engaging in the old, undesirable behavior, we can adopt a new, more pleasant routine. For example, if boredom triggers mindless scrolling, we may replace that habit with a more fulfilling activity, such as reading a book, going for a walk, or spending time with loved ones.

The reward component of the habit loop is equally significant. Understanding what we genuinely want when we engage in a habit allows us to create healthier and more sustainable ways to meet our needs. For example, if we use social media to connect with others, we could seek out in-person social contacts instead. If we are eating junk food to cope with stress, we should consider other stress-management approaches, such as exercise or meditation.

Breaking harmful behaviors is difficult, but not impossible. By actively disrupting the habit loop and substituting old habits with new ones, we may rewire our brains and effect long-term change. Establishing new brain pathways requires time and effort, so patience and persistence are essential. However, with persistent practice and a willingness to explore, we may break free from our old habits and develop new ones that align with our aims and beliefs.

Understanding the habit loop is especially important while trying to achieve our goals in a distracted society. Many of the diversions we experience are caused by habits. For example, the persistent desire to check our phones or refresh our social media feeds is frequently a deeply rooted habit reinforced by the dopamine rush of likes, comments, and notifications.

We may begin to break free from these distractions by recognizing them as habits. We can identify the triggers, change our habits, and find healthier ways to meet our needs. This can lead to a more focused and intentional life in which we have control over our activities rather than being dictated by our habits.

Habit Stacking: Building Positive Routines

We frequently find ourselves drawn to the appeal of new habits. We see ourselves meditating every day, exercising frequently, reading more books, or learning a new skill. Despite our best efforts, these new behaviors frequently fail to take hold, slipping away as fast as they appeared. The difficulty in incorporating new behaviors into our already hectic lives is the real barrier, not the desire for change.

Fortunately, habit stacking is a powerful technique that has the potential to transform how we approach habit development. This clever strategy uses the strength of our established routines to create a smooth road for new habits to thrive. By deliberately matching new habits with established ones, we may capitalize on the momentum of our current behaviors, making it much simpler to incorporate beneficial changes into our everyday lives.

Habit stacking is a simple but efficient notion. It entails recognizing an existing behavior that you practice on a regular basis and then "stacking" a new habit on top of it. This leads to a chain reaction, with the completion of one habit automatically triggering the next. For example, if you already make your bed every morning, you may incorporate a new practice of stretching for five minutes right after. You establish a natural flow by connecting these two acts, which makes it easier to recall and practice the new habit.

Habit stacking's brilliance stems from its ability to harness the power of cues and associations. Our brains are hardwired to make associations between experiences and behaviors. When we frequently perform one action after another, our brains learn to correlate the two behaviors together. This association grows stronger with time, eventually becoming a habit.

By stacking a new habit on top of an old one, we effectively create a new cue for the new habit. The completion of the old habit acts as a reminder to conduct the new behavior, increasing the likelihood that we will follow through. This reduces the need to rely simply on willpower or motivation, which can be transient and ineffective.

To successfully apply habit stacking, it is critical to select the appropriate anchor habit. This should be a habit you already have and can accomplish with little effort. It should also be a habit that occurs at a time and location that is convenient for performing the new habit. For example, if you wish to start a daily meditation practice, you may incorporate it into your morning coffee ritual. After you finish your coffee, you would immediately sit down and meditate.

Once you've decided on your anchor behavior, the following step is to select the new habit you want to build on top of it. This might be any behavior that you desire to incorporate into your daily life, such as exercising, reading, or practicing appreciation. The trick is to adopt a small and manageable habit, which increases the likelihood that you will stick to it.

When creating your habit stack, be clear about the order of actions. Instead of just saying, "After I brush my teeth, I will meditate," try saying, "After I put my toothbrush away, I will sit on my meditation cushion and meditate for five minutes." This level of specificity aids in developing a clear and actionable plan.

It's also vital to start simple and progressively add to your habit stack. Avoid attempting to implement too many new habits at once, as this can be overwhelming and lead to burnout. Instead, concentrate on mastering one new habit at a time before attempting another.

As you gain confidence with habit stacking, you can begin to design more intricate chains of behaviors. For example, you may incorporate several habits into your morning routine, such as cleaning your bed, stretching for five minutes, meditating for five minutes, and having a glass of water. This establishes a powerful morning ritual that prepares you for a productive and focused day.

Habit stacking is a versatile method that can be used for a variety of purposes and situations. It can help you develop beneficial habits, increase productivity, reduce stress, and even fight procrastination. By utilizing the power of our current habits, we can make long-term changes in our lives and create a more focused and meaningful future.

So, if you're having trouble adopting new habits or making long-term changes, consider habit stacking. It's a simple yet powerful technique to tap into the power of your current routines and make long-term positive changes.

Self-Reflective Questions:

1. **Habitual Autopilot:** What are the top 3 habits I engage in daily without much thought? Are they hindering or helping my focus and goals? (Jot down your daily routines, especially those done mindlessly).
2. **Cue Awareness:** What triggers my most distracting habits? Are there specific times, locations, or emotional states that make me more prone to them? (Reflect on the situations where unwanted habits arise).

3. **Reward System:** What am I truly seeking when I engage in my habits? Is the reward fulfilling a genuine need, or is it a temporary fix masking a deeper issue? (Dig into the emotional/physical payoff of each habit).
4. **Focus-Friendly Habits:** What current habits already support my focus and productivity? How can I strengthen them or use them as building blocks for new, positive habits? (Identify existing routines that aid your focus and leverage them).
5. **Change Readiness:** On a scale of 1-10, how ready am I to change my most distracting habits? What barriers might I face, and how can I overcome them? (Assess your motivation and potential obstacles to change).

Transformative Exercises:

1. **Habit Tracker:** Create a visual tracker to monitor your habits for a week. Mark each day you successfully engage in a positive habit and note any triggers for negative habits. This provides a clear overview of your progress and potential areas for improvement.
2. **Cue Modification:** For a distracting habit, experiment with altering the cue. If it's your phone buzzing, put it on silent. If it's a specific location, change your surroundings. See how changing the trigger affects your urge to engage in the habit.

3. **Routine Replacement:** Choose one distracting habit and brainstorm alternative routines to fulfill the same underlying need. If it's stress eating, try a quick walk or deep breaths instead. Practice this new routine consistently for a week and observe the changes.
4. **Reward Substitution:** If your habit's reward isn't healthy, find a substitute. Instead of the dopamine hit from social media, reward yourself with a healthy snack or a few minutes of enjoyable activity after completing a focused work session.
5. **Habit Stacking Practice:** Choose an existing positive habit and stack a new, desired habit onto it. For example, after brushing your teeth (existing habit), do a quick meditation (new habit). This leverages the existing routine to make the new habit easier to adopt.

Chapter Ten: Mindfulness for Focus

The Present Moment: Anchoring Your Attention

Our minds jump from one thought to the next, lingering on the past or worrying about the future, rarely pausing to simply be in the present moment. The key to focus and fulfillment, however, resides in the present moment, the elusive "now."

Mindfulness, a practice with ancient roots in Eastern philosophy, provides a method to recover our attention and anchor it firmly in the present. It is a state of active, open attention to the present moment, with conscious awareness of our ideas, feelings, physiological sensations, and surroundings. Mindfulness is not about emptying the mind or repressing thoughts; rather, it is about witnessing our thoughts and feelings without judgment, allowing them to pass like clouds in the sky.

Mindfulness originated in ancient Buddhist traditions and was established as a sort of mental training to enhance awareness, compassion, and wisdom. In these traditions, mindfulness was viewed as a means of obtaining inner peace and release from suffering.

While mindfulness has its roots in Eastern philosophy, it has gained popularity in Western culture in recent decades. Its benefits have been extensively researched and recorded, with studies demonstrating that mindfulness can reduce stress, improve focus and concentration, improve emotional regulation, and even increase creativity.

In our distracted environment, mindfulness provides a potent antidote to the incessant draw on our attention. By training our minds to be more present, we may avoid the temptation to become engrossed in the never-ending stream of thoughts and distractions that assault us every day. Instead of obsessing on the past or worrying about the future, we can learn to completely engage in the present moment, relishing life's basic pleasures and finding clarity in the midst of confusion.

Focusing on the breath, observing bodily sensations, or paying attention to the sounds, images, and smells of one's surroundings are all common aspects of mindfulness practice. These activities help to focus our attention on the present moment and develop a stronger feeling of awareness.

One of the primary advantages of mindfulness is its potential to help us become more aware of our thoughts and emotions. When we are mindful, we can examine our thoughts and feelings without passing judgment, allowing us to recognize them for what they are: transient mental processes that do not define us. This non-reactive awareness enables us to approach situations with greater calm and resilience.

Mindfulness also helps us develop better self-compassion. When we are conscious, we may acknowledge our own suffering and treat ourselves with compassion and understanding. Self-compassion can help us heal from past hurts, overcome self-doubt, and develop a more positive self-image.

In addition to the personal benefits, mindfulness can improve our connections with others. When we are completely present with the people we care about, we can listen more profoundly, sympathize more fully, and connect more truly. This can result in deeper, more meaningful connections and a stronger sense of connectedness to the world around us.

Incorporating mindfulness into our daily lives does not have to be difficult or time-consuming. Even a few minutes of focused breathing or meditation every day can have a major impact. We can also incorporate mindfulness into our daily routines, such as eating, walking, and driving. We can develop a higher feeling of awareness and focus just by paying attention to the current moment and our body's sensations.

Meditation Techniques: Training Your Mind

Meditation, at its core, is the practice of honing our attention and awareness. It entails consciously focusing our minds on a certain object, such as the breath, physiological sensations, or a mantra, while letting go of any distractions or thoughts that emerge. While meditation can take various forms, each with its own focus and benefits, the basic idea stays the same: establish a condition of present-moment awareness.

Breath awareness. One of the most common and accessible types of meditation is to simply focus on your breath's natural rhythm. Find a comfortable seated position, either on the floor or in a chair, with your spine straight and your shoulders relaxed. Close your eyes or soften your gaze, and softly focus on the sensation of your breath as it enters and exits your nose or as your abdomen rises and falls. Consider the nature of your breath: is it shallow or deep, smooth or choppy? Observe any sensations relating to your breath, such as the coolness of the air entering your nostrils and the warmth of your breath leaving your mouth.

When thoughts emerge, as they will, simply acknowledge them without judgment and gently return your focus to your breathing. This technique of non-reactive awareness allows you to notice your thoughts and emotions without becoming engrossed in them. Regular practice will increase your capacity to focus and concentrate, both on and off the meditation cushion.

Another common meditation technique is body scanning. This exercise entails systematically directing your attention to various parts of your body and noting any sensations that arise. Scan your body gently, starting with your toes and progressing to your legs, torso, arms, and head. Take note of any sensations of stiffness, relaxation, tingling, or warmth. Like with breath awareness meditation, the key is to just watch these sensations without judgement and allow them to pass.

The body scan might be very beneficial for people who experience physical strain or pain. Bringing awareness to the body allows us to reduce tension and experience better comfort and ease. Furthermore, the body scan might help us feel more grounded and present by focusing our attention on the bodily sensations of the moment.

Loving-kindness Meditation, also known as Metta meditation, is the practice of fostering compassion and kindness for oneself and others. This technique entails repeating certain phrases or affirmations, such as "May I be happy," "May I be healthy," "May I be safe," and "May I live with ease." These statements can be aimed at yourself, family members, friends, strangers, or even difficult people in your life.

Loving-kindness Meditation can reduce stress, anxiety, and depression while increasing emotions of happiness, connection, and well-being. We can cultivate compassion and kindness towards ourselves and others, resulting in a more positive and helpful inner dialogue and more resilience in the face of adversity.

These are only a few of the various meditation techniques accessible. Experimenting with multiple ways is the greatest way to find a practice that feels right for you. There is no right or wrong way to meditate, and what works for one person may not work for someone else. The trick is to select a practice that you enjoy and can stick with on a regular basis.

Meditation has several benefits for improving focus. Regular meditation has been demonstrated to increase attention span, reduce mind wandering, and promote cognitive flexibility. It can also assist in alleviating tension and anxiety, both of which have been linked to poor focus and concentration.

Furthermore, meditation can boost self-awareness, allowing us to better comprehend our thoughts, emotions, and triggers, allowing us to make more deliberate decisions and avoid distractions.

Self-Reflective Questions:

1. **Present Moment Awareness:** How often do I find myself fully present in the moment, without judgment or distraction? What percentage of my day is spent on autopilot, dwelling on the past, or worrying about the future?
2. **Mind Wandering:** How often does my mind wander during tasks or conversations? What are the typical themes or patterns of my wandering thoughts? (Try to notice when your mind drifts away and gently guide it back to the present).
3. **Sensory Experience:** How often do I pause to truly notice my senses—the sights, sounds, smells, tastes, and textures around me? Am I fully experiencing my life through my senses, or am I missing out on the richness of the present moment?
4. **Emotional Awareness:** How comfortable am I with my emotions? Can I observe my feelings without judgment or reactivity, or do I tend to get swept away by them? (Start noticing the subtle nuances of your emotions as they arise and pass).
5. **Mindful Habits:** What aspects of my daily life could benefit from a more mindful

approach? Can I identify specific activities, such as eating, walking, or communicating, where I can practice being more present and engaged?

Transformative Exercises:

1. **Mindful Breathing:** Set a timer for 5-10 minutes and find a comfortable seated position. Close your eyes or soften your gaze and bring your attention to the natural flow of your breath. Notice the rise and fall of your abdomen, the sensation of the air passing through your nostrils, and the gentle rhythm of each inhale and exhale. Whenever your mind wanders, gently guide your attention back to your breath.
2. **Body Scan Meditation:** Lie down or sit comfortably and systematically bring your attention to different parts of your body, starting from your toes and moving up to your head. Notice any sensations you feel in each area, such as tingling, warmth, or tension. Simply observe these sensations without judgment, allowing them to come and go.
3. **Mindful Walking:** Go for a walk in a quiet place, such as a park or nature trail. As you walk, pay attention to the sensations of your feet touching the ground, the movement of your legs, and the feeling of the air on your skin. Notice the sights, sounds, and smells around you.

4. **Mindful Eating:** During your next meal, slow down and savor each bite. Pay attention to the flavors, textures, and aromas of your food. Notice the sensations of chewing and swallowing. Avoid distractions, such as watching TV or reading, and focus fully on the experience of eating.
5. **Mindful Listening:** During your next conversation, practice mindful listening. Give the other person your full attention, without interrupting or formulating your response. Notice their tone of voice, body language, and facial expressions. Try to understand their perspective and be fully present in the conversation.

Chapter Eleven: Stress Management

Stress and Focus: The Connection

We often underestimate the significant impact of stress on our ability to concentrate and achieve our goals. Stress, while a natural and often even healthy response to adversity, can quickly become a formidable foe if continuous and overpowering. Stress has far-reaching physiological consequences on the brain, decreasing cognitive function, interfering with focus, and eventually jeopardizing our general health.

When we are in a stressful situation, our bodies trigger a series of physiological responses that help us cope with the perceived threat. While the "fight or flight" response is necessary for survival in perilous situations, it can have a negative impact on our minds and bodies if it becomes a chronic condition.

Cortisol, a hormone produced by the adrenal glands, plays an important role in the stress response. Cortisol is essential for mobilizing energy and getting our bodies ready for action. However, persistent stress can cause cortisol levels to remain elevated for long periods of time, which can be harmful to our brains.

According to research, excessive cortisol levels can affect the functioning of the prefrontal cortex, which is responsible for executive processes such as decision-making, planning, and attention. This impairment can emerge in a variety of ways, such as trouble concentrating, poor memory, and decreased cognitive flexibility.

Furthermore, persistent stress can alter the structure and function of the hippocampus, a brain area responsible for learning and memory. According to studies, continuous stress can shrink the hippocampus, causing memory issues and increasing the likelihood of acquiring neurodegenerative disorders such as Alzheimer's.

Stress has a tremendous impact on our attention. When we are anxious, our attention shifts to the source of the stress, making it difficult to focus on other things. This can create a vicious cycle in which stress inhibits our capacity to focus, which leads to additional stress.

Chronic stress can also disturb the balance of neurotransmitters in the brain, including dopamine and serotonin, which are necessary for mood regulation and cognitive function. This can cause anxiety, despair, and irritation, worsening focus issues.

The relationship between persistent stress and attention issues is well recognized. According to studies, those who endure chronic stress are more likely to have difficulty concentrating, remembering, and making decisions. They are also more easily distracted and struggle to stay focused.

This can have a major impact on both their personal and professional lives. Students may fail to focus in class, resulting in low academic achievement. Professionals may have difficulty concentrating at work, resulting in lower productivity and missed deadlines. In the personal realm, stress-related attention issues can make it difficult to engage in meaningful conversations, connect with loved ones, and enjoy everyday activities.

The positive news is that we are not immune to the consequences of stress. Understanding the physiological mechanisms by which stress affects our brains allows us to devise techniques to counteract its harmful effects and regain our attention. This entails implementing stress-management practices such as mindfulness meditation, exercise, and spending time outdoors. It also entails living a more balanced and fulfilling life in which we prioritize our well-being and set aside time for leisure and enjoyment.

Stress Reduction Techniques: Finding Calm Amidst Chaos

While stress is a natural part of the human experience, it may be harmful to our health and pleasure if it persists and is not managed. It can take many forms, ranging from physical symptoms like headaches and exhaustion to emotional discomfort like anxiety and irritation. The positive news is that we are not helpless against stress. By incorporating effective stress-reduction strategies into our daily lives, we can not only reduce the negative impacts of stress, but also improve our overall well-being and reach our full potential.

Mindfulness practices, which are founded in ancient wisdom traditions, provide an effective antidote to the stress of modern life. Even in the midst of external chaos, we can cultivate present-moment awareness and nonjudgmental acceptance of our thoughts and feelings, creating a space of inner peace. Mindfulness meditation, for example, is focusing our attention on the present moment, monitoring our thoughts and sensations without becoming engrossed in them. This simple yet deep exercise can help to calm the mind, minimize rumination, and build a sense of inner peace.

Exercise is another excellent way to reduce stress. Physical activity has been demonstrated to significantly improve our mental and emotional wellbeing. When we exercise, our bodies release endorphins, which are natural substances that improve our mood and relieve pain. Exercise can also assist in lowering cortisol levels, a stress hormone that can have a negative impact on our bodies if it is consistently raised. Whether it's a brisk walk, a yoga class, or a high-intensity workout, finding an exercise that you love and can include into your daily routine can be an effective method to reduce stress and enhance your overall well-being.

Deep breathing exercises are another simple yet effective approach to relieve stress and promote relaxation. When we are stressed, we tend to breathe shallowly and rapidly. We may activate the body's relaxation response by purposefully slowing and deepening our breathing, which helps to lower heart rate and blood pressure and calm the nervous system. Diaphragmatic breathing is a simple method in which you breathe deeply into your abdomen, allowing it to expand as you inhale and contract as you exhale. This sort of breathing engages the diaphragm, a major muscle that helps regulate our breathing and can induce a state of peace and relaxation.

Spending time in nature has also been demonstrated to have a major stress-reducing effect. According to studies, spending time in nature can reduce cortisol levels, lower blood pressure, and boost mood. Simply spending time in a park, forest, or other natural area can help to calm the mind, reduce anxiety, and create feelings of peace and well-being. Connecting with nature, whether through a leisurely walk in the woods, a picnic in the park, or simply sitting by a lake and admiring the scenery, can be an effective method to recharge and de-stress.

Finally, finding social support is an important part of stress management. Connecting with friends, relatives, or a therapist can give a secure environment in which to express our burdens, get perspective, and receive emotional support. Talking about our worries might help us release pent-up emotions and feel less isolated and overwhelmed. Furthermore, social support can create a sense of belonging and connection, which is critical for our well-being.

Self-Reflective Questions:

1. **Stress Inventory:** What are the primary sources of stress in my life? Are they related to work, relationships, health, finances, or

other factors? (Make a list of your stressors to gain clarity on their origins and impact).
2. **Stress Signals:** How does my body react to stress? What physical or emotional symptoms do I experience when I'm feeling overwhelmed or anxious? (Pay attention to your body's signals, such as muscle tension, headaches, fatigue, or changes in appetite or sleep).
3. **Coping Mechanisms:** How do I currently cope with stress? Are my coping mechanisms healthy and sustainable, or do they exacerbate the problem? (Be honest about your coping strategies, such as overeating, excessive alcohol consumption, or social withdrawal).
4. **Stress Threshold:** What is my stress threshold? How much stress can I handle before it starts to negatively impact my focus, productivity, and well-being? (Recognize your personal limits and the point at which stress becomes overwhelming).
5. **Stress-Relief Practices:** What activities or practices help me to relax and de-stress? How often do I engage in these activities, and could I benefit from incorporating more stress-relief practices into my routine? (Identify activities that promote relaxation and well-being, such as exercise, meditation, or spending time in nature).

Transformative Exercises:

1. **Mindfulness Meditation:** Set aside 10-15 minutes each day to practice mindfulness meditation. Find a quiet space, sit comfortably, close your eyes, and focus on your breath. Notice the sensations of your breath entering and leaving your body, and observe any thoughts or feelings that arise without judgment.
2. **Progressive Muscle Relaxation:** Lie down in a comfortable position and systematically tense and relax different muscle groups in your body, starting from your toes and working your way up to your head. This can help to release physical tension and promote relaxation.
3. **Gratitude Practice:** Each day, write down three things that you are grateful for. This could be anything from a supportive friend to a beautiful sunset. Focusing on gratitude can help to shift your perspective and cultivate a more positive outlook.
4. **Nature Immersion:** Spend time in nature regularly. Go for a walk in the park, hike in the woods, or simply sit by a lake and enjoy the scenery. Research has shown that spending time in nature can reduce stress, improve mood, and boost creativity.
5. **Social Connection:** Make time for meaningful social interactions with friends, family, or colleagues. Share your thoughts and feelings with trusted loved ones, or

simply enjoy their company. Social connection can provide a valuable source of support and help to reduce feelings of isolation and loneliness.

Chapter Twelve: Sleep and Focus

Sleep Deprivation: The Focus Killer

We frequently sacrifice sleep because we believe that working late will help us achieve our goals. However, this mistaken belief could not be further from the truth. Sleep is neither a luxury nor a sign of laziness; it is a fundamental biological necessity that is critical to our physical and mental health. It is the foundation of cognitive function, influencing our ability to pay attention, remember, make decisions, and maintain mental clarity. In a society filled with distractions that require our continual attention, understanding the science of sleep and the negative impacts of sleep deprivation is critical for anybody who wants to focus and achieve their goals.

Sleep is more than just a condition of inactivity; it is an active process in which our minds and bodies perform necessary restorative activities. During sleep, our brains consolidate memories, analyze information, and heal cellular damage. Sleep also helps regulate our hormones, immune system, and metabolism. In essence, sleep serves as the foundation for both our physical and mental wellness.

When we don't get enough sleep, our cognitive abilities degrade. Sleep deprivation has been frequently proven in studies to decrease concentration, memory, and decision-making ability. Sleep deprivation makes it more difficult to concentrate, slows reaction times, and reduces our capacity to think effectively and creatively. We are also more likely to make mistakes and poor decisions because our brains do not operate optimally.

The effect of sleep deprivation on attention is very substantial. Sleep regulates the brain chemicals that control our alertness and focus. When we are sleep deprived, these molecules become imbalanced, making it difficult to concentrate, stay focused, and avoid distractions. This can be especially harmful in a world where distractions abound and our attention is continually drawn in several directions.

Sleep deprivation has a substantial impact on another cognitive function: memory. During sleep, our brains consolidate memories, moving them from short-term to long-term storage. When we don't get enough sleep, this process is disturbed, making it difficult to develop new memories and recall previously taught information. This can have a substantial impact on our capacity to learn new skills, perform well at work or school, and make sound judgments.

Sleep deprivation also impairs decision-making capabilities. When we are sleepy, we are more prone to making rash decisions based on emotion rather than reasoning. We are also less capable of assessing risks and weighing the possible outcomes of our decisions. This can result in poor decision-making in both our personal and professional lives, which can have major implications.

Chronic sleep deprivation, defined as continuously sleeping less than our bodies require, might have much more serious repercussions. Over time, it can raise the chance of acquiring a variety of health issues, including obesity, diabetes, heart disease, stroke, and certain types of cancer. Sleep deprivation can also damage our immune system, leaving us more vulnerable to infections and illnesses.

Chronic sleep deprivation can have a negative impact on both our physical and mental health. Sleep deprivation has been related to an increased chance of developing depression, anxiety, and other mood disorders. It can also worsen pre-existing mental health disorders, making them more difficult to treat.

Furthermore, prolonged sleep loss can have an adverse effect on our relationships and social interactions. When we are weary and angry, we are less likely to be patient, understanding, or compassionate to others. This might result in disagreements, misunderstandings, and a breakdown in communication.

Sleep Hygiene: Optimizing Your Sleep for Peak Performance

Sleep hygiene refers to a variety of routines and behaviors that promote restful sleep and optimal daytime alertness. By applying these measures, we may increase our sleep quality, boost our cognitive function, and accomplish our goals more easily and efficiently.

One of the most important parts of sleep hygiene is maintaining a consistent sleep pattern. This involves going to bed and waking up at the same time every day, including weekends. Our bodies have an internal clock called the circadian rhythm, which controls our sleep-wake cycle. Maintaining a consistent sleep pattern allows us to align our circadian rhythm with our daily activities, making it simpler to fall asleep and wake up feeling refreshed.

Developing a soothing bedtime ritual is another important aspect of sleep hygiene. This entails slowing down in the hours before bedtime and engaging in activities that promote relaxation and prepare the body for sleep. This could include taking a warm bath, reading a book, listening to soothing music, or practicing relaxation techniques like deep breathing or meditation. Avoiding stimulating activities like watching TV or working on the computer in the hours before bedtime can also help with sleep quality.

Optimizing your sleeping environment is another important component of getting restful sleep. Your bedroom should be dark, quiet, and chilly, as these are the optimal sleeping conditions. Investing in blackout curtains, earplugs, or a white noise machine can help create a more relaxing and sleep-friendly atmosphere. Additionally, ensure that your mattress and pillows are comfy and supportive, as this can have a big impact on your sleep quality.

Addressing common sleep problems is also critical to improving sleep hygiene. If you have trouble falling asleep, remaining asleep, or waking up feeling groggy, you should see a doctor. Common sleep disorders, such as insomnia, sleep apnea, and restless legs syndrome, can have a major influence on both sleep quality and general health. Identifying and treating these illnesses can result in significant improvements in sleep and overall well-being.

In addition to these fundamental principles of sleep hygiene, there are several other actionable strategies that can help you enhance your sleep quality:

- **Avoid caffeine and alcohol before bedtime**: caffeine and alcohol can disrupt sleep, making it difficult to fall and remain asleep. Avoid these substances in the hours before bedtime.
- **Limit your daytime naps**: Short naps are refreshing, but long or frequent naps might impair your nocturnal sleep. If you need to nap, make it short (20-30 minutes) and avoid resting late in the afternoon.
- **Get frequent exercise**: Regular exercise can enhance sleep quality, but exercising too close to bedtime can make it difficult to fall asleep.
- **Manage stress**: anxiety and worry can disrupt sleep. Relaxation practices, such as meditation or deep breathing, can help reduce stress and induce relaxation before sleeping.
- **Seeing the light**: Getting enough natural light during the day can help you regulate your circadian cycle and sleep better. Make sure you get some sunlight every day, especially in the mornings.
- **Create a sleeping haven**: Make your bedroom a calming and pleasant environment. Keep it clean, uncluttered, and at a pleasant temperature. Invest in comfy

bedding and pillows, and avoid using electronic gadgets in your bedroom.

By adopting these sleep hygiene habits into your daily routine, you can improve your sleep and reap a variety of benefits, including increased attention, productivity, happiness, and general health.

Self-Reflective Questions:

1. **Sleep Quantity:** How many hours of sleep do I typically get each night? Is this amount sufficient for my age and activity level, or am I consistently sleep-deprived? (Track your sleep for a week to get an accurate assessment of your sleep duration).
2. **Sleep Quality:** How would I rate the quality of my sleep? Do I fall asleep easily and stay asleep throughout the night, or do I wake up frequently feeling unrested? (Reflect on how rested you feel upon waking and throughout the day).
3. **Daytime Alertness:** How alert and focused do I feel during the day? Do I experience energy slumps, difficulty concentrating, or irritability due to lack of sleep? (Pay attention to your energy levels and cognitive function throughout the day).
4. **Sleep Disruptions:** Are there any factors that regularly disrupt my sleep, such as caffeine consumption, alcohol use, screen time before bed, or a noisy sleep

environment? (Identify potential sleep disruptors in your routine and environment).
5. **Sleep-Related Health Issues:** Have I experienced any sleep-related health issues, such as insomnia, sleep apnea, or restless leg syndrome? If so, have I sought professional help or explored treatment options? (Consider whether underlying sleep disorders may be contributing to your sleep problems).

Transformative Exercises:

1. **Sleep Schedule Consistency:** Establish a consistent sleep schedule by going to bed and waking up at the same time each day, even on weekends. This helps to regulate your body's natural sleep-wake cycle and improve sleep quality.
2. **Bedtime Routine Creation:** Create a relaxing bedtime routine to wind down before sleep. This could include activities such as reading a book, taking a warm bath, listening to calming music, or practicing relaxation techniques like deep breathing or meditation. Avoid stimulating activities like watching TV or using electronic devices in the hour before bed.
3. **Sleep Environment Optimization:** Make your bedroom a sleep sanctuary by optimizing your sleep environment. Ensure that your room is dark, quiet, and cool. Invest in blackout curtains, earplugs, or a

white noise machine if needed. Make sure your mattress and pillows are comfortable and supportive.
4. **Sleep Tracking:** Use a sleep tracker app or wearable device to monitor your sleep patterns. These tools can provide valuable insights into your sleep duration, quality, and any potential disruptions. Use this information to identify areas where you can improve your sleep hygiene.
5. **Professional Consultation:** If you are experiencing chronic sleep problems or suspect that you may have a sleep disorder, consult with a healthcare professional. They can help you diagnose any underlying issues and recommend appropriate treatment options to improve your sleep quality.

Chapter Thirteen: Focus in Relationships

Mindful Communication: Being Present with Others

Mindful communication is founded on the concepts of mindfulness, the practice of paying attention to the present moment without judgment. It entails paying full attention to the interaction, actively listening to what the other person is saying, and reacting with empathy and compassion. This style of communication goes beyond words to include nonverbal indicators, emotional undercurrents, and unsaid messages that are often hidden beneath the surface.

Active listening is a key component of mindful communication. It requires us to be fully present, engaged, and attentive to the speaker's message, rather than simply hearing what they are saying. Active listening entails paying attention to the speaker's tone of voice, body language, and facial expressions, in addition to the content of their words. It also includes asking clarifying questions, summarizing what we've heard, and reflecting on the speaker's feelings.

By actively listening, we show the speaker we value their opinions and are interested in their thoughts. This fosters trust and safety, enabling the speaker to feel heard and understood. Active listening also allows us to obtain a better grasp of the speaker's point of view, resulting in more meaningful and effective talks.

Being fully present in conversations is another important aspect of mindful communication. In today's distracted environment, it is simple to let our minds wander during discussions, thinking about other things, checking our phones, or planning our next response. However, when we are not fully present, we miss the conversation's nuances and the chance to connect, too.

To be fully present in a conversation, we must develop the ability to silence our internal dialogue and focus our attention on the speaker. This includes putting aside our phones, turning off any distractions, and making eye contact with the speaker. It also entails letting go of our own agenda and remaining open to what the other person has to say.

Empathy is the ability to comprehend and share the emotions of others. It is a critical component of mindful communication because it enables us to connect with others on a deeper, emotional level. Empathy allows us to put ourselves in the shoes of others and see the world from their point of view. This allows us to better grasp their motives, concerns, and needs.

Empathy is more than simply cognitive understanding; it also includes emotional resonance. When we are fully sympathetic, we can sense what the other person is feeling. We understand their delight, grief, fury, and terror. This common emotional experience forges a strong link between people, encouraging trust, compassion, and understanding.

Empathy requires us to be sensitive and open to others' emotions. It also needs us to be nonjudgmental and open to diverse points of view. When we approach interactions with empathy, we are more likely to overcome understanding gaps, resolve issues amicably, and form deeper connections with those around us.

Mindful communication is about enhancing not only our connections with others but also our relationship with ourselves. Increasing our awareness of our own thoughts, feelings, and communication patterns can provide us with significant insights about our own needs, motivations, and triggers. This self-awareness can help us communicate more effectively, have healthier relationships, and live more rewarding lives.

In a society filled with distractions, mindful communication is an effective tool for regaining our concentration and developing deeper connections with people. By actively listening, remaining completely present in conversations, and exercising empathy, we may tear down boundaries, encourage understanding, and build a more compassionate and connected society.

Setting Boundaries: Protecting Your Time and Energy

Boundaries are not barriers that separate us from others; rather, they are rules that govern how we interact with the world, helping us to maintain positive relationships, prioritize our needs, and protect our most valuable resources: time, energy, and attention.

Imagine your life is a garden. Without boundaries, it becomes overgrown and chaotic, with weeds choking out the exquisite flowers and fruits that you've meticulously created. Similarly, if we do not set boundaries in our relationships, we risk becoming overloaded, overextended, and tired, leaving us with little energy or attention for what actually matters.

Setting appropriate boundaries does not imply being selfish or unkind; rather, it entails acknowledging and conveying our own limits to others. It is about saying "yes" to things that are consistent with our beliefs and ambitions and "no" to things that aren't. It's about creating a personal and professional growth environment.

In our personal relationships, boundaries help us establish and communicate our own wants and preferences to those we care about. They allow us to set limits on how much time and energy we are willing to contribute to others while still leaving enough for ourselves. This is especially crucial in close relationships because the distinction between our own wants and the needs of others can readily blur.

Setting boundaries in personal relationships can include saying "no" to requests you don't have time for or that don't align with your values, limiting your time with certain people, and assertively communicating your needs and expectations. Establishing and maintaining appropriate boundaries allows us to build relationships that are mutually respectful, helpful, and gratifying.

In our work life, boundaries are just as vital. They assist us in protecting our time, energy, and focus from the relentless pressures of work. Without boundaries, we can easily get overwhelmed with emails, meetings, and other work-related responsibilities, leaving little time or energy for our personal lives.

Setting boundaries in the workplace can entail a variety of strategies, including communicating clearly with colleagues and managers about your availability, establishing designated work hours, and learning to say "no" to requests that are outside of your scope of responsibility or would overload your schedule. It may also include building a physical and digital workspace that reduces distractions and increases focus.

By setting and maintaining workplace boundaries, we may foster a more productive and fulfilling work environment. We can also reduce stress, avoid burnout, and maintain a work-life balance.

Establishing boundaries can be difficult, especially if we are not used to demanding our needs or saying "no." However, with practice and determination, it may become a natural and empowering part of our daily lives. It's crucial to remember that setting limits isn't about being perfect; it's about making deliberate decisions that reflect our values and objectives.

Setting successful limits requires clear and aggressive communication. This is stating your wants and expectations in a straightforward and courteous manner, without apologizing or offering excuses. It also requires respecting your limits and saying "no" to loved ones.

It is also critical to be flexible and adaptable when it comes to boundaries. Our needs and priorities can shift over time; therefore, our boundaries may need to be adjusted accordingly. The goal is to be aware of our own needs and convey them to others in a way that is courteous and successful.

By creating and keeping appropriate boundaries in our personal and professional relationships, we can safeguard our time, energy, and attention, allowing us to achieve our objectives, nurture our well-being, and live a more full life. In a society that is constantly demanding our attention, the capacity to set boundaries is a superpower that can help us construct a really unique life.

Self-Reflective Questions:

1. **Present Presence:** When interacting with loved ones, how often am I fully present, not just physically, but mentally and emotionally? Do I find my mind wandering to other tasks or concerns? (Reflect on specific interactions where your attention might have wavered).
2. **Listening Quality:** Am I truly listening when others speak, or am I just waiting for

my turn to talk? Do I actively try to understand their perspective, or am I quick to judge or offer solutions? (Evaluate your listening skills and how they impact your relationships).
3. **Device Distraction:** How often do I interrupt conversations or shared moments to check my phone or other devices? Do I prioritize digital interactions over real-life connections? (Assess the role technology plays in your interpersonal relationships).
4. **Emotional Connection:** How deeply do I connect with others on an emotional level? Am I able to express my feelings openly and honestly, and am I receptive to the emotions of others? (Reflect on the depth and authenticity of your emotional connections).
5. **Relationship Boundaries:** Do I have healthy boundaries in my relationships that protect my time, energy, and focus? Do I communicate my needs clearly and respectfully, or do I tend to overextend myself? (Evaluate the balance of give and take in your relationships).

Transformative Exercises:

1. **Phone-Free Time:** Designate specific times each day or week for phone-free interactions with loved ones. Put away your devices and engage in activities that promote connection and conversation, such as

sharing a meal, going for a walk, or playing a game together.
2. **Active Listening Practice:** During your next conversation, make a conscious effort to practice active listening. Give the other person your undivided attention, make eye contact, and use verbal and non-verbal cues to show that you are engaged in what they are saying. Reflect back their feelings and ask clarifying questions to ensure understanding.
3. **Empathy Enhancement:** Choose a person you care about and try to see the world through their eyes. Consider their experiences, perspectives, and challenges. Imagine how they might be feeling and try to understand their motivations and actions. This exercise can help you cultivate greater empathy and compassion.
4. **Digital Detox in Relationships:** Plan a digital detox with your partner, family, or friends. Agree to disconnect from your devices for a specific period, such as a weekend or a few hours each day. Use this time to connect with each other on a deeper level, engage in shared activities, or simply enjoy each other's company.
5. **Boundary Setting:** Identify one area in your relationships where you need to establish clearer boundaries. This could be related to time, energy, personal space, or communication. Communicate your needs clearly and assertively to the other person,

and practice saying "no" when necessary. Remember, healthy boundaries are essential for maintaining healthy relationships.

Chapter Fourteen: Focus at Work

Deep Work: Creating Flow States for Productivity

Cal Newport developed the term "deep work" in his renowned book of the same name. It refers to the habit of focusing without distraction on a cognitively challenging job. It is a state of flow in which we are completely involved in our jobs, devoid of the distractions of continual interruptions and superficial busywork. In a society that bombards us with stimuli and demands our attention at all times, deep work provides a haven of focus and productivity.

To grasp the actual potential of deep work, we must first recognize the superficial work that consumes our days. Shallow work is defined as jobs that are low-value, repetitive, and easily copied. These actions, such as checking email, attending useless meetings, or scrolling through social media, may provide the impression of being busy, but they rarely produce real results. Shallow labor fragments our attention, depletes our mental energy, and hinders us from participating in deep thinking, which is required for creativity, invention, and problem solving.

Deep work, on the other hand, serves as an antidote to shallow work. It is the ability to focus without distraction on a cognitively demanding endeavor. This could include producing a complex report, evaluating data, creating a new product, or devising a novel solution to a difficult problem. Deep work is difficult; it involves discipline, focus, and the willingness to withdraw from the continual barrage of distractions that surround us. However, the benefits of lengthy labor are enormous.

When we do profound work, we are able to realize our entire cognitive capacity. We can think more clearly, solve issues more efficiently, and develop more innovative ideas. We can also feel more satisfied and fulfilled at work since we are making real progress toward our goals.

So, how can we create settings in our lives that encourage profound work? The first step is to reserve certain periods of undisturbed time. This is setting up specified times in your day or week to focus entirely on a single topic without distractions. This could include marking off time on your schedule, turning off notifications, silencing your phone, and locating a quiet workspace where you can work uninterrupted.

The duration of these intensive work sessions will vary according to your personal preferences and the nature of the task at hand. Some people believe that shorter, more frequent sessions are more effective, whereas others favor longer, less frequent sessions. The trick is to experiment and discover a rhythm that suits you.

To get the most out of your deep work sessions, create rituals and habits that help you transition into a focused state. This could include listening to relaxing music, doing a quick meditation, or simply taking a few deep breaths. It's also beneficial to have a clear goal in mind for each session and divide your activity into smaller, more manageable chunks.

Dealing with interruptions is an unavoidable aspect of intense labor. Even with the best intentions, our thoughts may wander and external disruptions will occur. The goal is to develop skills for managing distractions and swiftly regaining attention.

Creating a distraction list is an effective method. Whenever a distracting thought or concept enters your mind, write it down on your list and return to it later. This enables you to acknowledge the notion without becoming distracted by it.

Another option is to take short rests in between deep work sessions. This can help you avoid mental tiredness and stay focused for extended periods of time. During your pauses, you can stand up and move around, stretch lightly, or just take a few deep breaths.

It's also crucial to be aware of your energy levels. Deep work demands a lot of mental energy, so plan your sessions around times when you are most awake and focused. For many people, this occurs early in the morning or following a brief respite.

Managing Interruptions: Staying on Track

In the fast-paced symphony of the modern office, interruptions are a constant refrain that may easily break the balance of focus and productivity. Whether it's a chatty coworker, an unexpected meeting, or a flood of emails, these interruptions can divide our focus, impede our productivity, and leave us feeling stressed and unproductive. While interruptions are an unavoidable aspect of professional life, we are not powerless to counteract their disruptive effects. Effective interruption management tactics can help us regain our attention, protect our productivity, and create a more fulfilling work experience.

Colleagues, while an important element of any job, may also be a significant source of distraction. A simple question here, a polite interaction there, and before you know it, precious minutes have turned into hours of wasted productivity. Establishing clear limits and expectations is critical for dealing with interruptions from colleagues. This may entail scheduling defined times for collaboration and individual work, communicating your availability to others, and politely but firmly denying disruptions when you need to focus. Consider employing visual indicators, such as headphones or a "Do Not Disturb" sign, to communicate to your coworkers that you are deep in work and should not be bothered until absolutely necessary.

Meetings, while frequently required for collaboration and decision-making, may also be a significant time sink. Back-to-back meetings can leave us exhausted and unproductive, leaving little time for focused work. To reduce the influence of meetings on your focus and productivity, choose which meetings to attend carefully. Consider whether your presence is truly necessary or whether the information might be transmitted via another channel, such as email or a shared document. If you do attend a meeting, be prepared with a clear agenda and goals, and actively engage to ensure that the group continues on track and meets its objectives.

Emails, while a useful mode of communication, can soon become overwhelming and distracting. The steady flood of communications can divide our attention, disrupt our workflow, and instill a sense of urgency that is tough to dismiss. To avoid email distractions, schedule regular times during the day to monitor and react to emails, rather than checking them continually. You may also use filters and rules to automatically arrange your emails into folders, allowing you to prioritize and respond to the most important communications first. Consider unsubscribing from newsletters and promotional emails you don't read, and utilize your email client's "Do Not Disturb" feature to turn off notifications during focused work periods.

Other job distractions, such as phone calls, office noise, and social media, can all disrupt our focus and productivity. To address these distractions, consider utilizing noise-canceling headphones to create a quieter work environment, putting your phone on silent mode, and employing website blockers to prevent yourself from visiting distracting websites during work hours. You can also set aside a specific workspace free of distractions, such as a quiet corner of the office or a separate room.

In addition to these specific tactics, it is critical to build a comprehensive approach to interruption management. This entails being aware of your own energy levels and attention span, setting realistic goals for yourself, and taking pauses when needed. It also entails explaining your demands to others and establishing boundaries to safeguard your time and attention.

Self-Reflective Questions:

1. **Work Environment Assessment:** How conducive is my current work environment to focus and deep work? Are there specific aspects of my workspace or office that regularly distract me? (Consider lighting, noise levels, clutter, and proximity to colleagues).
2. **Interruption Frequency:** How often am I interrupted during my workday? What are the primary sources of these interruptions (e.g., colleagues, emails, meetings)? How much time do I typically lose to these interruptions? (Track interruptions for a day or two to get a clear picture).
3. **Focus Blocks:** Do I schedule dedicated blocks of time for focused work? If so, how effective are these blocks at minimizing distractions and allowing me to engage in deep work? (Reflect on your current scheduling practices and their impact on your focus).
4. **Communication Patterns:** How do I communicate my need for focus to colleagues and managers? Do I set clear boundaries around my work time, or am I easily accessible and prone to interruptions? (Consider how you can improve communication around your focus needs).
5. **Work-Life Integration:** How well do I integrate my work life with my personal life? Do I have clear boundaries between work

and leisure time, or do I find myself constantly checking emails and responding to messages outside of work hours? (Reflect on how your work habits impact your personal life and vice versa).

Transformative Exercises:

1. **Workspace Optimization:** Identify specific changes you can make to your workspace to minimize distractions and enhance focus. This could involve decluttering your desk, adjusting lighting, using noise-canceling headphones, or relocating to a quieter area.
2. **Deep Work Schedule:** Block off specific times in your calendar for deep work sessions. Communicate your availability to colleagues and managers, and avoid scheduling meetings or other commitments during these dedicated focus blocks.
3. **Interruption Management:** Develop strategies for managing interruptions. This could involve setting office hours for colleagues, batching email responses, or using a "Do Not Disturb" sign to signal your need for uninterrupted work time.
4. **Focus Rituals:** Create a pre-work ritual to help you transition into a focused mindset. This could involve a short meditation, a few deep breaths, or reviewing your goals for the day. You can also create a post-work ritual to

help you disconnect from work and transition into your personal time.
5. **Tech-Free Zones:** Establish tech-free zones in your life, both at work and at home. This could involve designating certain areas as device-free, such as your bedroom or dining room, or setting specific times of day when you disconnect from technology.

Chapter Fifteen: The Focused Life

Beyond Productivity: The Benefits of Focus

Beyond productivity, there is a wide range of benefits that affect our creativity, decision-making, well-being, and overall sense of purpose. By embracing the power of focus, we can live a deeper, more rewarding life that goes beyond ticking boxes and meeting deadlines.

Creativity, that elusive spark that ignites creativity and propels progress, flourishes on the rich ground of attention. When we are fully engaged in a task or endeavor, our brains might wander, find connections, and explore new possibilities. This state of deep focus allows us to access our subconscious mind, which is typically where creative concepts and solutions live. Consider the numerous breakthroughs and innovations that have resulted from periods of peaceful thought and undisturbed focus. From Einstein's theory of relativity to the invention of the iPhone, many of humanity's greatest triumphs have emerged from the depths of concentrated attention.

Focus enhances decision-making, which affects every aspect of our lives. In a world inundated with information and opinions, the capacity to filter out noise and focus on the most important aspects is critical. When we are focused, we can examine information more critically, weigh alternatives more thoroughly, and make decisions that are consistent with our beliefs and goals. This clarity of thought can improve our personal and professional lives.

Focus is more than just a fuel for creativity and decision-making; it is also a key component of well-being. When we are totally involved in an activity that we enjoy or find meaningful, we reach a state of flow, a condition of effortless focus in which time appears to disappear and we become entirely immersed in the present moment. This state of flow is not only delightful, but it is also extremely restorative, lowering stress, improving mood, and improving overall well-being.

Furthermore, focus can help us develop a stronger sense of mindfulness, which is the discipline of paying attention to the present moment without judgment. We can escape the cycle of rumination and worry that plagues our minds by learning to focus our attention on the present moment. This can result in increased self-awareness, emotional regulation, and a stronger sense of inner calm.

Focus is also important in shaping our sense of purpose. When we can direct our energy and attention toward our passions and ideals, we are more likely to have a feeling of purpose and fulfillment in our lives. This sense of purpose may be a strong motivator, inspiring us to overcome obstacles, pursue our aspirations, and make a positive difference in the world.

In a world full of distractions, establishing attention is not simply an issue of productivity but also of living a deeper, more meaningful life. We may achieve our maximum potential and live a successful and satisfying life by learning to quiet the noise, tune out distractions, and direct our attention to what truly matters.

Attention's benefits extend far beyond the workplace to all aspects of our lives. Whether we want to advance our careers, strengthen our relationships, or simply enjoy the present moment, focus is the key that opens the door to a more satisfying and meaningful life.

Creating a Life of Intention: Your Path to Fulfillment

Creating a life of intention is a transforming journey that allows us to explore our inner landscape, clarify our beliefs, and make deliberate decisions that reflect our true selves. It is a process of self-discovery in which we uncover our passions, aspirations, and desires and align our activities with our core values. Living intentionally allows us to build a sense of purpose, meaning, and contentment that goes beyond the transitory pleasures of a distracted society.

The first step to living a life of intention is to visualize your ideal life. Consider how your life might be different if you had complete control over it. What would you do? Who would you spend time with? Where would you live? What kind of impact would you have on the world?

This activity is not about constructing a fantasy world that is impossible or unrealistic. It's about discovering your greatest passions and aspirations and using them to guide you on your journey. By visualizing your perfect life, you may start to determine the exact goals and values you wish to prioritize.

Once you have a clear picture of your ideal existence, the next stage is to match your behaviors with those beliefs. Values are guiding concepts that influence our actions and behaviors. Our values define us and what we stand for. By connecting our behaviors with our values, we can live a life that is genuine and fulfilling.

To match your activities with your values, first define your basic values. What are the most essential aspects of your life? Is it honesty, integrity, kindness, imagination, adventure, or something else? Once you've discovered your basic principles, think about how you may use them in your daily life. How can you make personal and professional decisions that reflect your values?

For example, if one of your fundamental values is creativity, you could schedule time each day for creative activities like writing, drawing, or playing music. If adventure is one of your key values, you could arrange regular vacations or outings to explore new places and do new things.

Aligning your behaviors with your principles is a continual process that necessitates continuous awareness and reflection. It is about making intentional decisions that are consistent with your innermost beliefs and objectives. When your behaviors are consistent with your beliefs, you will experience a higher feeling of purpose, meaning, and fulfillment in your life.

Focused living is another important component of an intentional life. In a world that is constantly competing for our attention, it's common to feel disorganized and overwhelmed. By building focus, we may concentrate our energy and attention on what is genuinely important, allowing us to achieve our goals and live a more full life.

Focused living means setting clear goals and making deliberate decisions about how to spend our time and energy. It entails saying "yes" to things that are consistent with our values and ambitions, and "no" to distractions and time wasters that divert us from our true path.

To cultivate focus, we can use a range of tools, including mindfulness meditation, time management approaches, and creating a distraction-free atmosphere. We can also set limits on technology, prioritize sleep and exercise, and engage in activities that nourish our minds and bodies.

By may create a rich, meaningful, and fulfilling life by living consciously and focusing on what actually matters. We may stop the pattern of distraction and live a life that is truly our own.

Self-Reflective Questions:

1. **Life Satisfaction:** On a scale of 1-10, how satisfied am I with my life overall? Which areas of my life bring me the most joy and fulfillment? Which areas could be improved? (Reflect on your overall happiness and identify specific areas that you would like to enhance).
2. **Value Alignment:** How well do my daily activities and choices align with my core values? Am I living a life that is congruent

with my deepest beliefs and aspirations? (Assess whether your actions reflect your values and identify any discrepancies).
3. **Personal Growth:** Am I actively pursuing personal growth and development? What new skills or knowledge would I like to acquire? What steps can I take to expand my horizons and reach my full potential? (Consider setting goals for personal growth and creating a plan to achieve them).
4. **Contribution:** How am I contributing to the world around me? Am I making a positive impact on my community, family, or the environment? How can I use my talents and skills to make a difference? (Reflect on your contributions and consider how you can make a greater impact).
5. **Life Purpose:** What is my overarching purpose in life? What legacy do I want to leave behind? What kind of person do I want to be remembered as? (Explore your deeper sense of purpose and meaning in life).

Transformative Exercises:

1. **Ideal Life Visioning:** Create a vision board or write a detailed description of your ideal life. Include aspects such as your career, relationships, health, hobbies, and personal development. Visualize yourself living this life and feeling the emotions associated with it.

2. **Values Clarification:** Make a list of your core values. Then, review your calendar and daily activities to see how well they align with your values. Identify any areas where you can make adjustments to better reflect your values in your daily life.
3. **Personal Growth Plan:** Set specific goals for personal growth and development. This could involve learning a new skill, taking a course, reading books on a particular topic, or attending workshops or seminars. Create a plan with actionable steps to achieve your goals.
4. **Contribution Project:** Identify a cause or issue that you are passionate about and find a way to contribute to it. This could involve volunteering your time, donating money, or using your skills and expertise to support a cause that you believe in.
5. **Life Purpose Exploration:** Spend some time reflecting on your life purpose. What are you passionate about? What unique gifts and talents do you have to offer the world? How can you use your skills and experience to make a difference in the lives of others?

www.ingramcontent.com/pod-product-compliance
Lightning Source LLC
Chambersburg PA
CBHW071927210526
45479CB00002B/591